The Ultimate Wealth-Maker

By **T.J. Rohleder,** Founder of the Direct-Response Network
and
Chris Lakey, Marketing Director of the
Direct-Response Network

This book is dedicated to Russ von Hoelscher, the man who took my wife and partner, Eileen, and I by the hand and helped us make millions of dollars in our first four years.

Thank you, Russ!

TABLE OF CONTENTS

INTRODUCTION

by T.J. Rohleder

This small book you are holding in your hands really is the ultimate wealth maker. In fact, as you will soon see, this amazing opportunity has the true wealth-making power to give you all of the money you want and need for the rest of your life! Best of all, the total cost for this ultimate way to get massive amounts of money for life is yours for only...

$3.41 a day.

Yes, for about the cost of a deluxe fast-food hamburger or taco meal, you can get the amazing tips, tricks, strategies, and personal help, support, and guidance that truly does have the powerful ability to make you super rich for the rest of your life!

Does all of this sound too good to be true? Probably... **But it's not!**

Listen closely. I don't blame you for being skeptical about everything I just said. But as you'll see, all five of the powerful benefits you will read about in the 5 Chapters of this small book really do have the amazing power to make you all of the money that you'll ever want and need for the rest of your life!

Here's The Amazing Secret.

This book gives you the proven secrets behind our new Platinum Membership in our Direct-Response Network. The D.R.N. is a revolutionary new Company that combines the power of network marketing with five additional multi-billion-dollar marketing methods. Our product line is a special Membership that's made up of products and services that are carefully designed to make all of our Members (and the Distributors who offer our Memberships) massive sums of money with the same strategies and proven methods that our parent Company (M.O.R.E. Incorporated) has used to generate over $100-Million Dollars in direct marketing sales within our first 19 years!

We have many different products and services that are designed to help our Members become financially set for life! But none of them is greater than the five main Member benefits you will receive when you become a Platinum Member of the D.R.N.

So, if you really are serious about making the maximum amount of money in the minimum amount of time — you must quickly go through this small book and then become a Platinum Member today! Each Chapter was written by myself and my marketing director, Chris Lakey, to tell you a little bit about each of the 5 main Member benefits you will receive when you become a Platinum Member.

As you will see, any one of these 5 main benefits could potentially make you rich. But together, they have even more wealth-making power! Go over this book and prove this to yourself! Then, go to the special Web-Site on the bottom of every other page in this book — and print out the Platinum Membership Application Form that you will find on the Web-Site. Just fill out this Form and mail or FAX it to us — and you can begin receiving all five of these ultimate wealth-makers for _less_ than the cost of a deluxe hamburger or taco meal at one of those greasy-spoon fast-food restaurants.

Sincerely,

T.J. Rohleder
Goessel, Kansas

From: Chris Lakey, Marketing Director of the D.R.N....

FOR FUTURE PLATINUM-LEVEL MEMBERS ONLY...

Let Us Do Our Best To Help You Get Rich!

"Come Inside and Join Us As A Charter Member Of Our Private Inner-Circle Group — So We Can Do Our Best To Help You Get Rich."

How many great things could you do and how much more money could you make _if_ you had a rags-to-riches millionaire and his entire staff working for you?

Here's your unique NO-RISK opportunity to rip the ceiling off your earning power.

If you want the help of one of America's most celebrated millionaire-makers... If you want to stay home and create a home-business that could make you rich... And if you're one of the first to respond to this limited offer, you can start off with our valuable

<u>FREE</u> gifts worth $12,223.50!

THIS IS THE ULTIMATE WEALTH-BUILDING BREAKTHROUGH!!

Getting personal and private help from a millionaire-maker is the key-secret that has made T.J. Rohleder (the co-founder of our company, 'M.O.R.E. Incorporated) rich. I know — beyond a doubt — it can make you rich, too. In fact, this is the proven road to wealth.

America's first billionaire, J.P. Getty, said it best when he said:

"<u>No</u> <u>One</u> <u>Gets</u> <u>Rich</u> <u>By</u> <u>Themselves</u>."

Here's T.J.'s quick story to prove this...

In the early 80s, T.J. Rohleder and his wife, Eileen, were on a quest to get rich... They were desperately searching for a way to build wealth... They wanted all the good things that money could buy... The nice home, shiny new cars, exotic vacations, freedom, security, etc.

So they began to buy every plan they could get their hands on...

Soon their mailbox was STUFFED with dozens of sales letters from all kinds of people who promised to help them get rich... They bought all the money-making plans that looked different. Most were junk. They weren't even worth the paper they were printed on...

But a few of the money-making plans were different.

In fact, one of the Programs they sent for really worked! <u>Soon</u> <u>they</u> <u>were</u> <u>making</u> <u>hundreds</u> <u>of</u> <u>dollars</u> <u>a</u> <u>week</u>! They made the

---

plan even better... <u>And even more money rolled in</u>. It was so exciting...

Then they had a major discovery!

T.J. and Eileen knew there had to be thousands of people — just like them — who were searching for a simple and easy way to make money. And most of the plans and programs were garbage... ***But their plan really worked!*** *"Why not share this with other folks?"* they asked. *"We can make our money — by helping them make more money."*

THEY WENT FROM ZERO TO $16,000.00 A MONTH!

Soon they were selling their proven plan to other people just like them... THEIR LIVES WERE INSTANTLY CHANGED! They began making money by helping others make money...

Before long, T.J. and Eileen were making more cash than they ever dreamed possible... around $16,000 a month! It was amazing!

Then their lives changed again...

Then they met marketing expert Russ von Hoelscher... Russ is one of America's top wealth-creating Consultants. He saw their first ad... and wrote to tell them how much he liked what they were doing...

Russ offered to give them several of his greatest secrets. They spent some time on the phone with Russ and then paid him $<u>2,500.00</u> to spend a couple days sharing his most closely guarded get-rich secrets! Russ pulled out all the stops... He gave them dozens of proven strategies that they could put to immediate use.

And his secrets worked like magic! **Within 9 months, they were making almost $100,000.00 a week...** Over the following year, they paid Russ many thousands of dollars for his personal consulting and help... **And they joined his Inner Circle to get ongoing help and support.**

With Russ's help, T.J. and Eileen went from making about $16,000 per month in sales... to up to $100,000.00 per week in the first 9 months! And he's helped them make tens of millions since then...

That's how **I know** that getting personal help — and having a private friendship with people like Russ von Hoelscher can...

HELP YOU GET SUPER RICH!

And now for the best news!! Now you can get the same type of help that made T.J. and Eileen millions of dollars. *IN FACT...*

You Can Let T.J. And Our Staff Do Our Best To Help You Get Super Rich For The Low Price Of Only $3.41 A Day.

IT'S TRUE! Now, you will get the benefits of Membership in our Private Inner Circle that is designed to make you rich! This is the ultimate wealth-making Coaching Program the world has ever seen!

It's called:

"THE $100-MILLION DOLLAR SYSTEM COACHING PROGRAM!"

This is your once-in-a-lifetime opportunity to join now and get the benefits of Membership in our Inner Circle Group!

Together, self-made millionaire T.J. Rohleder, with the help of his hand-picked staff, will do the very best to personally and privately help you make all the money you want — for as long as you want it!

Just think of what this can mean to you:

America's #1 Blue-Jeans Millionaire-Making Expert Will Do His Very Best To Help You Get Rich!

By joining our new "*$100-MILLION DOLLAR SYSTEM COACHING PROGRAM!*" You will get the powerful benefit of letting T.J. Rohleder and our hand-picked staff help you with the same tips, tricks, strategies, and THE EXACT TURN-KEY EASY-TO-USE SYSTEMS that have brought us...

Over $100-MILLION DOLLARS in *less* than 18 years!

Our Inner-Circle group is designed to help you become financially free.

We have developed this group to help a small exclusive number of our best Clients and Customers earn the largest amount of money possible.

This group is powerful. Your life (and finances) can be transformed forever. As a Member of our group, you'll get the personal help, support, guidance, and secret methods that we are now using to make a fortune.

The main things that separate the winners from the losers in this world are the friends you keep and the people you know! You'll have a powerful FRIEND in the business who will help you every step of the way.

This is so important to your ultimate success — I must say it

---

Self-employed people make up less than 20 percent of the workers in America but account for two-thirds of the millionaires.

Dr. Thomas Stanley and Dr. William Danko
"The Millionaire Next Door"

Keep away from people who try to belittle your ambitions. Small people always do that , but the really great let you know that you, too, can become great.

Mark Twain

to you again and again...

It's not always _what_ you know. It's _who_ you know — _and who you're getting your personal help from_ — that can help you get rich.

Do you want financial freedom? Then start by associating with others who are _already_ rich.

This is a true wealth secret that can change your life.

This secret made T.J. Rohleder millions of dollars. I know in my heart that it can make YOU rich, too.

Here's the God's-Honest Truth: T.J. Rohleder would not be a multi- millionaire today — if it wasn't for Russ von Hoelscher. **Russ became his friend in the business.** Russ was the one who took T.J. and Eileen by the hand and showed them the way to get rich... Russ was the friend who told them exactly what to do and how to do it... Russ is the person who gave them his private contact list that helped them even more... Russ is the one who guided them... He revealed the secret to getting Mailing Lists of people who would love to buy what we sell... **He gave them — in just a short period of time — what had taken him over 20 years to discover!** He told them what to do.. And, even more important, he told them what _not_ to do...

Russ became their close friend and 'coach' in the business — and that made all the difference in the world... It can make all the difference to you, too.

That's the secret to having a successful Mentor... and now you can have T.J. Rohleder, myself, and our hand-picked staff as your personal Mentors, working for you day in and day out!

You need successful friends and mentors. WHY?

<u>Because</u>...

You will <u>never</u> get rich by yourself.

You need the help of successful people who started broke — and have gone on to making huge sums of money... You need friends who have done it. These are the only people who can truly help you make money.

<u>You need friends who believe in you when nobody else does</u>.

****

You need experts to call on when you need help... You need a super successful team of winners who will show you how to make the largest sum of money — in the fastest time... You need people who truly care about your success... You need people who want to help you... <u>You need people who have been where you are — and found the way out</u>... You need all the rich friends you can find — who are making a ton of money — and will do their best to help you make your fortune.

****

And this is what we will do for you! T.J. and his handpicked team of staff members will help you use our greatest secrets you can use to build wealth...

Now you can rub shoulders with a true Mail-Order and Internet Marketing Expert and his hand-picked and well trained staff, including me, who can help you get rich... You'll go behind the scenes as we reveal our inner-most secrets for making huge amounts of cash and give you all the personal help and support you need and deserve!

Together, T.J. Rohleder with the help of me and our key staff members have brought in over one hundred million

dollars in less than 18 years. And now we want to help YOU get rich!

Just like you, T.J. did not start with the Silver Spoon in his mouth.

T.J. comes from humble beginnings... He knows how it feels to struggle for every dollar... He started broke or with very little and went on to making a fortune (with a lot of help from our talented staff). Now he wants to extend his hand to you — to help you make all the money you want.

You'll Get Our Personal Help And the Secrets We Used to Turn The Small Sum of $300.00 in Cash into over $100-Million Dollars in our first 18-years... We'll show you exactly what to do and how to do it to make the most money possible.

You'll Receive our personal help, support, guidance, and proven time-tested million-dollar ideas! All of us will be there to help you every step of the way.... Whenever you need us — we'll be there for you. You'll get our personal help and guidance 365 days a year. **WE WILL BE YOUR FRIENDS IN THE BUSINESS!**

You'll Get The USA's Top "Blue Jeans Millionaire" Rags-To-Riches Wealth-Building Expert And His Well Trained Staff Helping You Make Money For Four Full Years!

You'll get the personal help of one of the very best get-rich experts and his well trained staff, for four full years!

Together, all of us will show you exactly what to do and help you make the most money possible.

This Coaching and Mentoring Program is a bargain at its regular price of only $500.00 a month... Why? Because — **just a** few of the ideas you can get from being a Member in this private group could potentially make you an easy $100,000.00 a year — or much more! (But don't worry, you're *NOT* going to pay anywhere near $500.00 a month...)

You're In The Right Place At The Right Time.

Today's new technology makes it possible for anyone, even people with just a little money or almost no money, to compete head to head with well established gigantic businesses and win!

But, to make your home business a success, you've got to keep up with all the newest secrets. You must stay on top of the latest cutting-edge methods for getting rich.

That's where we come in.

You can potentially get rich with our personal help. You see, every successful person I know of had a mentor who watched over them, guided them, and handed down their wisdom to make sure these wealthy people reached their fullest potential...

And we're excited about having YOU as an elite Charter Member of our "*$100-MILLION DOLLAR SYSTEM COACHING PROGRAM!*" Why? Because we know you're serious about making huge sums of money. We can't wait to help you do it!!

You'll Start By Getting Our Private Collection Of 2,267 Pages Of Hard-Core Wealth Secrets!

We have spent many years and hundreds of thousands of dollars to discover these SIMPLE, but amazingly powerful secrets. They virtually guarantee success in any home-based business. These secrets have made us, and a small group of others, millions of dollars. We know they have the powerful potential to make you

---

a fortune, too.

And remember, we will be there to personally help you.

There's not enough room to give you all 598 MILLIONAIRE-MAKER SECRETS... However, here's a list of just a few of our closely-guarded secrets that (along with the personal help and support) will now be yours:

#15   **EASILY PROTECT YOUR BEST IDEAS! Everything you need to know about copyrights, trademarks, and patents...**

#22   **Four _easy ways_ to turn your ideas into instant cash.**

#55   **How to make up to $100 profit for every $10 you spend!**

#74   **How to find dirt-cheap products that sell like crazy!**

#75   **_Five Easy Steps_ That Guarantee Your Success.**

#80   **Four proven ways to instantly increase your profits overnight.**

#132   **Instantly make 3-TIMES MORE MONEY by doing one small thing.**

#138   **THE SMART WAY To Make Money Starting From Zero.**

#149   **How To Make Thousands Of Extra Dollars C Without Lifting A Finger!**

#161   **How to increase your profits by up to 1,000%.**

#162   **The Perfect Way To Make A Lot Of Money After You Retire.**

#185   **The Four Little-known Steps To Become A Millionaire.**

Minds are like parachutes: they only function when open.

Thomas R. Dewar

Work and love – these are the basics. Without them, there is neurosis.

Theodor Reik

When all think alike, then no one is thinking.

Samuel Goldwyn

#207 The 5-Minute Trick To Turning Small Ads Into BIG Money.

#284 <u>The secret key to making up to $1,000,000 a year or more in selfpublishing.</u>

#288 What is the 'hottest subject ever' that could make you $1,000,000 a year?

#311 *How To Earn Steady Money All Year Long.*

#325 The safest and most profitable way to make money.

#426 *How Joint Ventures Can Bring You Riches.*

#437 How to let other people's marketing secrets make you rich.

#447 How To Prosper Faster Than You Ever Thought Possible.

#450 *How to make BIG PROFITS with NO INVESTMENT!*

#455 4 Ways To Make Your Ads Pull BIG MONEY.

#483 How To Make As Much Money As You Want For The Rest Of Your Life.

#492 How To Increase Your Profits By 1,000% to 10,000%.

#512 15 Ways To Guarantee Your Product Will Sell By Mail!

#514 Four Little Things That Radically Boost Your Income.

#571 How two hours a day can help you make $20,000 a week!

#573 A million dollar secret formula to getting TOTALLY FREE Advertising!

#579 *The fast way we turned $1,000 into $10,000,000...*

#581 The secret to making up to $500,000 a year with newspapers.

#585 *How to choose the perfect name for your new company!*

#590 *The simple way to set up your own business in 1 hour... legally.*

#598 A simple 30 page report could make you $250,000+ a year!

These are just some of the SECRET METHODS that you'll get when you become a Member of our "*$100-MILLION DOLLAR SYSTEM COACHING PROGRAM!*"

These ultimate secrets are for our "*$100-MILLION DOLLAR SYSTEM COACHING PROGRAM!*" only. We'll RUSH this giant 2,267 page collection to you the same day we receive your Platinum Membership Application Form.

Best of all, we'll help you cash in with them. You'll use these secrets with us looking over your shoulder. We'll be there to help you cash in with them. We'll make them super easy for you. We'll show you the short-cut way to make a mint with our 598 hidden secrets.

But that's not all! No way! Not by a long-shot...

You'll get our personal and private help for four full years. PLUS, You start with our valuable FREE Bonus Gift worth $12,223.50 that you can keep even if you decide this isn't perfect for you — PLUS, you'll also receive MORE FREE GIFTS worth the full, but absolutely true value of over $250,000.00!!

With our private help — you can get more money than you ever dreamed possible. You can have the good things only money can buy... The big home, luxury car, second home, exotic vacations, and plenty of spendable cash to make all of your dreams come true.

Listen closely. You'll <u>never</u> be truly free in western society without money... It takes money to live your dreams and help the people you love and want to help... It takes money to pay all your bills each month — with plenty left over afterward. **It takes money — and lots of it — to do all the things you've always wanted to do.**

<u>You</u> <u>know</u> <u>this</u> <u>is</u> <u>true</u>.

Isn't it time to do something great for yourself and your future? This can happen as a Member of our "*<u>$100-MILLION DOLLAR</u> <u>SYSTEM</u> <u>COACHING</u> <u>PROGRAM</u>!*" You'll get our full help, support, and guidance. Getting the personal help from all of us can help you to a fortune. This is no guarantee that you will get rich — however, as you've seen — we have the knowledge and experience to help you turn your dreams of riches into reality.

You see, every successful person has a mentor or coach who watches over them, guides them, and hands down their wisdom to make sure these people reach their fullest potential.

THE PROBLEM: A lot of people *claim* they can help you get rich. But how many of them are already rich? <u>The</u> <u>answer</u> <u>might</u> <u>shock</u> <u>you</u>. You see, many of the consultants and wealth experts we have investigated have never made any significant money for themselves... How in the world can they help you prosper? They can't. And you know it.

And that brings me to the #1 success rule:

The only people you should listen to are those who have already been successful accomplishing exactly what you are seeking to accomplish.

This is why you must join T.J. Rohleder's private group.

T.J. Rohleder And His Hand-Picked Staff Can Help You Get Rich In Mail-Order And On The Internet Like No Other Experts.

Simply put, there isn't anyone in the world today better able to guide you through the 'money-making jungle' — and help you achieve the personal wealth you desire and deserve.

Here's Why:

(1) **No one has our unique combination of making over $100-MILLION DOLLARS in less than 18 years! Remember, T.J. started with only $300.00... And he has taught us EVERYTHING he knows... Together, we will do our very best to help you get super rich!**

(2) **No one understands the newest secrets to getting rich in the 21ˢᵗ Century like we do. We stay on top of all the new high-tech secrets for making money. And we'll personally help you cash in with the newest technologies for maximum profit.**

(3) **No other group has been successfully helping other people make money for over 18 years like we have. And there's nowhere else where you can get the kind of help we will give you — for the low fee of $3.41 a day.**

Listen closely. Clients have gladly paid T.J. Rohleder up to $4,985.00 — and even more than that — for a couple of days of our money-making advice. T.J.s usual rate for personal one-on-one consulting is normally $1,000.00 an hour… *honest!!*

BUT YOU WON'T PAY OUR REGULAR FEES. Now

you can have the full help, support, and guidance of T.J. Rohleder, myself, and our hand-picked and well-trained staff Members — by your side, leading you through all the twists and turns of Mail-Order and the Internet's ever-changing landscape, pointing out the fruit and giving you all the information you need to pick it with the least effort by becoming a Member of our new and ultra private "*$100-MILLION DOLLAR SYSTEM COACHING PROGRAM!*"

We will give you our full help, support, and guidance. We know the secrets to building wealth. In fact, we've made millions of dollars thanks to our proven secrets. <u>That's how I know we can help you become rich, too</u>.

T.J. Rohleder, a.k.a. *"America's Blue Jeans Millionaire"* — along with myself, and our well trained staff, will give you our personal and private help. We'll help you make money with our time-tested secrets that have the potential to make you a small fortune from home.

You will see how simple and easy it is to make all the money you want from the comfort of your home. Now you can be an elite Member of our "*$100-MILLION DOLLAR SYSTEM COACHING PROGRAM!*" **You can potentially make a fortune with our personal help and proven secrets!**

THE <u>FIRST</u> WAY WE HELP YOU GET RICH —

"24-Hour Access."

You'll get <u>UNLIMITED ACCESS</u> to self-made millionaire T.J. Rohleder, myself, and his best hand-picked and trained staff members, "24 hours a day," for four full years, to answer your questions, offer hands-on help and support, and point out new trends and ideas to help you get rich. *YES! All of us will be <u>by your side</u> "24 hours a day."* **You can... contact us anytime, day or night. And your message will go <u>straight</u> to us. We'll give you our**

One good head is better than a hundred strong hands.

Thomas Fuller, Gnomologia, 1732

Most people don't manage to the utmost of their ability because they don't want to.

Robert Heller, The Super Managers, 1984.

Only the educated are free.

Epictetus, Discourses, ca. 100

ultra-private contact information.

Listen closely. We would like to personally help more people... MILLIONS want to get rich. And making huge sums of money is T.J. Rohleder's #1 passion in life... But, unfortunately, his time is **s-t-r-e-t-c-h-e-d to the limit**. He has us working on many different projects, developments, and innovations, too — and there's just <u>not</u> enough time in the day to personally help more people.

Few people have access to T.J. Rohleder's ultra-private contact information. <u>NOW YOU WILL BE ONE OF THEM</u>.

The private contact numbers you'll receive when you join our new "*<u>$100-MILLION DOLLAR SYSTEM COACHING PROGRAM!</u>*" are reserved for our closest friends and associates. <u>And now — you'll be one of these people.</u>

<u>**You will have "24-hour access" to us.**</u> With a few exceptions, during normal business hours, no matter where we are — or what we're doing — we will PERSONALLY get your messages and deliver our time-proven, knowledgeable, and qualified response in no time flat!

THE <u>SECOND</u> WAY WE HELP YOU GET RICH —

The "$100-MILLION DOLLAR High-Income Bible"

This 'bible' is for our "*<u>$100-MILLION DOLLAR SYSTEM COACHING PROGRAM!</u>*" Members only. In it — you'll discover all of OUR ULTIMATE 598 CLOSELY GUARDED SECRETS.

These are the ultimate methods, secrets, and strategies to build your fortune. All 598 of these closely guarded secrets have been

---

bound together into our 'bible'... We call it our 'bible' because it's that important to us.

> ***To the Christian, the Holy Bible is the most sacred book in the world (as it should be)...*** *And to those who want to get rich from home, our '$100-MILLION DOLLAR High-Income Bible' is the most sacred of all money-making books. You're going to cherish this special 'bible.'*

This is the 'bible' for all serious wealth seekers. You'll find yourself referring to it every single day. And each time you open it up you'll find all kinds of new ways you can make rich profits.

But that's not all... The '$100-MILLION DOLLAR High-Income Bible' is the main way we'll help you make the largest amount of money from home. You'll have your set of these CONFIDENTIAL materials close by you when you let us help you. And we'll be happy to go through it together to help you make money with our ultimate secrets!

*This is **the simple and easy way** we can personally help you get rich.*

This HUGE 2,267 PAGE 'bible' is our secret to helping you get rich from the comfort of your home. It's the most important wealth-building tool you can use to gain the riches you seek. And we will do our utmost to help you get rich with this special tool. You'll get our full support, help, and guidance. Best of all, you'll get it YOUR WAY. T.J. Rohleder and all of us will personally and privately help you get rich with the High-Income Secrets you love the most.

So do yourself a favor: Go take another quick look at a few of the 598 ultimate secrets. These are the same exact secrets — Plus many more — we'll be using to personally help YOU get rich.

THE __THIRD__ WAY WE HELP YOU GET RICH —

You Will Receive A Four Year Subscription To T.J.'s '$100-MILLION DOLLAR BOOTCAMP Audio Newsletter.'

As you know, recently we celebrated a major milestone. We hit a total of over $100-MILLION DOLLARS IN SALES, in _less_ than 18 years! It was a great achievement. After all, T.J. started with $300.00 in 1988 and now, less than 18 years later, brought in over $100,000,000.00!

So, to celebrate this historic event, T.J. decided to hold a series of special 'BOOTCAMPS' for his *"$100-MILLION DOLLAR SYSTEM COACHING PROGRAM!"* Members who want to make their fortune with the 26 main secrets that took us from $300.00 to over $100-MILLION DOLLARS in less than two decades. You are invited to attend at least one (and perhaps many!) of these events... FREE!

However, even if you can't make it to Kansas, you'll still receive the best of the best from these valuable wealth-making events — EVERY MONTH — Free!

These are the most powerful wealth secrets in history. Best of all, you will get them absolutely free! I will take the audio recordings of some of the best-of-the-best of these '$100-MILLION DOLLAR BOOTCAMPS' and re-package them into this very special monthly 'audio newsletter' that will contain many hours of the A-to-Z Wealth Formula!

This gives you a very special monthly audio program that has been carefully designed to make you a millionaire in no time flat! The regular price of this powerful money-making newsletter is $375.00 a year, but you'll get four years...FREE!

This powerful Coaching Program gives you...

On-Going Personal Help, Support, And Guidance
To Help You Build Your Personal Fortune!

Now you'll have 'a millionaire friend in the business' and his well trained staff members that you can count on. YOU'LL RECEIVE access to all of our personal and private contact information so you can reach us 24 hours a day — 7 days a week!

We can help you get rich like NOBODY Else Can. We'll do our best to help you get rich in Mail-Order and on the Internet. As you know (*IF* you read this entire letter)... we will do everything possible to privately help you make all the money you want.

As you can see — this FIRST Platinum Member Benefit alone has the power to make you huge sums of money!

But wait... there's more!

In fact, our '$100-MILLION DOLLAR COACHING PROGRAM' is only the beginning of everything you will be receiving!

So please read on — as we tell you all about the other very special wealth-making benefits you will receive when you become a Founding Member!

The NEXT SECTION was written by our Founder, T.J. Rohleder, to tell you all about THE SECOND PLATINUM MEMBER BENEFIT you will receive when you join this exciting top-level position.

Please read closely.

The things T.J. has to share with you will shock and amaze you. As you'll see — this 2nd Platinum Member Benefit alone has the amazing power to make you a multi-millionaire! *Read on*...

From: T.J. Rohleder, Founder of the D.R.N....

PLATINUM MEMBER BENEFIT #2

You Will Be One Of Only 20 Or Less Members — To Attend Our Famous 2-Day $3,985.00 Advanced Wealth-Making Workshops!

PLUS, YOU GET SPECIAL "ALUMNI STATUS" TO ATTEND UP TO 40 MORE OF THESE VALUABLE WORKSHOPS!!!

Hello, this is T.J. Rohleder — and I have some exciting news for you that could make you more money than you have ever dreamed possible!

Here's what it's all about...

I'm writing this segment of this book to tell you all about **THE SECOND very valuable Platinum Member Benefit** of the Direct-Response Network. As Chris Lakey said:

"This one benefit alone has the power to make you a multi-millionaire!"

Is this a guarantee or promise that you 'will' quickly become a multi-millionaire? <u>NO</u>. I cannot and will not promise you millions of dollars or any specific sum of money. **However, as you will see,** *the potential to make millions of dollars is definitely here!*

Here's how: This SECOND Platinum Member Benefit lets you attend up to 40 of the most powerful wealth-making workshops in history!

As you'll see, coming to these special Workshops can make you rich!

We held our first wealth-making Seminar in 1990... Since then, we have hosted dozens of these seminars. *The purpose of each event:*

TO <u>SHOW</u> <u>YOU</u> <u>HOW</u> TO <u>TURN</u> <u>SMALL</u> <u>SUMS</u> OF <u>MONEY</u> <u>INTO</u> <u>A</u> <u>GIANT</u> <u>FORTUNE</u>!

Our best Clients have gladly invested up to $6,850.00 to come to Kansas and attend our famous Seminars. Now we are holding a series of advanced wealth-making Seminars that are valued at $3,985.00 each... But you will attend as many of these events as you with — for no extra fee.

Yes, you will gain entry into these special events in Kansas that will give you the greatest secrets that took us from $300.00 to over $100,000,000.00 in total sales — in our first 18 years!

These events can change your life!

We're pulling out all the stops!

We plan to make each event more powerful than other Millionaire-Making Seminars that we have sold for $6,850.00! **And you can attend the next event that will be held in just a few weeks!**

But that's not all...

You see, when you become a Platinum Member — *you will also receive*...

FREE "ALUMNI STATUS" TO ATTEND ALL OF OUR VALUABLE WORKSHOPS!!!

We plan to hold DOZENS of our 2-day advanced wealth-making Seminars over the next 4 years... And YOU will have the opportunity to attend up to 40 of them... at no extra cost!

At $3,985.00 each this is a true value of up to $159,400.00!

Why should you attend as many as 40 of these wealth-making seminars? That's simple. You see, each time you come, you'll be getting new tips, tricks, and strategies that could potentially take you to the next level and make you many millions of dollars!

Best of all, now...

You and only 19 other people are invited to attend one of these special wealth-making Workshops that's coming up very soon.

All you do is come to Kansas. My staff and I will take it from there. We'll work with you and help you learn how easy it can be to make huge amounts of money in Mail-Order and on the Internet!

You'll discover how my wife, Eileen, and I started with a little over $300.00 and turned it into over ten million dollars in our first 4 years and over $100-Million Dollars to date... My staff (who is my second family) will work with you. We will answer all of your questions. We will be completely honest with you and show you what it really takes to make a fortune in your own Mail-Order or Internet Business!

I promise that, when you leave this event, you will have a whole new understanding about this amazing business of Mail-Order and Internet Marketing that I know you are interested in.

Why I'm Limiting This Wealth-Making Workshop To Only 20 Members And Their Guests...

I just got off the phone with one of my friends who told me I was <u>crazy</u> to only allow 20 of my Members to come to our special workshops and then let them come back for no extra charge... **He said I'd lose hundreds of thousands of dollars**... PLUS, he warned me that many of my Members would be very upset with me if they wanted to come but couldn't because all 20 seats were already filled.

So I thought about it. I know he's right... I know that I'll lose a lot of money by only inviting 20 people, but that's okay — because...

I'm Not Doing This Just For The Money!!

I decided to have these small cozy workshops in our office because I want to do something for our best Members. <u>I know that you are a lot like me because you are interested in making money from home</u> and I want to give you the personal help that you need.

I know that if I let a whole bunch of people come, I wouldn't be able to spend much time getting to know you and finding out how my staff and I could best help you... So I decided to keep these workshops very small and only invite YOU and 19 other Members. By doing that, I know that we can give you the most help!

As you may know, I've held Seminars with hundreds of people in attendance from all over the nation. Some of these events had so many people that we couldn't possibly get to know any of them personally. It's good for business but bad for us personally because there are so many wonderful people at these big events...

I still like to have big Seminars and they have their advantages (we can bring in other expert speakers to make the event more valuable, for one). But I made up my mind that I need to also have small and cozy workshops that would give my staff and me a chance to really get to know the people who came. We'd be able to find out what we could do to help them the most...

THIS IS GOOD NEWS FOR YOU!!! **Because you are invited to attend our next workshop! Just fill your Platinum Membership RIGHT NOW and you can be one of only 20 of my D.R.N. Members who can attend our next very special 2-day wealth-making workshop!**

To make this fair for everyone, I had to send this letter out to all of our D.R.N. Members and Clients... I didn't want to miss anybody who really needed to come and get our help... So you must become a Platinum Member now — to attend the next wealth-making workshop that will be coming up very soon!

What Can You Expect At These Warm And Personal 2-Day Millionaire Training Workshops?

First of all, one of my key staff members will be at the hotel (that is right next to the airport) to pick you and a guest up and take you to my headquarters in Goessel.

I skate to where the puck is going to be, not where it has been.

Wayne Gretzky

Fooling around with alternating current is just a waste of time. Nobody will use it, ever. It's too dangerous. Direct current is safe.

Thomas Edison

Wisdom comes by disillusionment.

George Santayana

On the first morning, my staff will be waiting for you in the lobby to take you on the 45-minute drive to our headquarters in Goessel.

Once you arrive, we'll ROLL OUT THE RED CARPET FOR YOU! We'll start by getting to know you... We will ask you what it is that we can give you by the time you leave... We will find out some of the questions you have and how we can help you get on the right track...

Then, I'll tell you our story... I'll tell you exactly how we started with a few hundred dollars and went on to making millions of dollars in our Mail-Order business in less than 4 years... I promise to be candid and completely honest. I'll tell you what we did right and some of the mistakes we made along the way. I'll give you our secrets that have brought us many tens of millions of dollars... *AND ALL OF YOUR BIGGEST QUESTIONS WILL BE ANSWERED!*

Then we will give you a tour of our headquarters... We will show you what we do, how we do it, and why... And we'll answer every question you have about our operation and what it "really" takes to run a successful Mail-Order and Internet Business.

I'll spend TWO FULL DAYS with you — to give you the bare essentials of what you need to get rich.

By taking TWO FULL DAYS to give you our greatest Mail-Order experiences you will be able to learn from what we have done right, as well as from the mistakes that we have made. I know this will help you avoid making the same mistakes that we have made, and I know that you will be able to learn a lot about what "really" works... And what "really" doesn't work...

All of the self-made millionaires I know are very busy people... They have a lot of money-making projects going on all the time and they don't like to be interrupted on the telephone. They especially don't like being interrupted by someone who could end up being a competitor of theirs someday!

Most of these people are far too busy making money for themselves in their successful Mail-Order Businesses to help you make any money.

Yes, I'm very busy, too... I have about 2 years worth of projects on my schedule of things that we want to do with our company. But I want to do something special for you and to really help you. I know that you are interested in making huge sums of money and I will give you the straight facts about making a fortune in your own home-based business. That's why I am inviting you and 19 other new Members to our next small and personal workshop that will be held very soon... then come to as many as 39 more of these events!!!!

Remember, I will show you <u>exactly</u> what we did to make all of our money — And give you a personal step-by-step plan that you can follow to start making your own Mail-Order and/or Internet fortune. I promise that you will leave these 2-day workshops with all of your wealth-making questions answered!

The difference between the right answer and the wrong answer can make you a lot of money! **Good information can make you rich and I promise that my staff and I will give you nothing but good information on all of the things that have helped us make millions of dollars.** I feel very confident that if we can do it — then you can do it, too! I only say this because I am a very average person. You will find that out when you meet me in person.

W-A-R-N-I-N-G: Don't Dress Up When You Come To These Special Seminars!

Some people have fancy seminars where the hosts come dressed in tuxedos and fancy suits. This will be NOTHING like that. We are keeping these very laid back and very relaxed!

Some people have lavish seminars where they try to show-off and "dazzle" all of the people who come and they really try to pump the people up with their glossy presentations. **We will not do this.** Our seminars will be very informal and we will not try to entertain you. But I guarantee: if making a lot of money is something that really excites you... *then you will have the best time of your life!*

I don't want you to dress up when you come to our seminars. I want you to relax. I want you to be natural and be yourself. And I promise to do the same thing for you! After all, this is one of the reasons that my wife and I are known as:

'The Blue Jeans Millionaires!'

We started our Mail-Order Business so we could do what we wanted to do when we wanted to do it. And this business has let us do just that!

My wife and I are a down to earth Midwestern couple. We don't like to dress up for things. **I REFUSE TO WEAR A TIE!** I hate wearing a suit. I feel most comfortable wearing Levi's Jeans and Nike Tennis Shoes... Most of my staff is the exact same way... We will not put on any "airs" with you. We will dress the way we normally dress and act the way we normally act. *"Whatcha see is whatcha get!"*

When you meet me and my staff in person you will find us to be very friendly, very average people. And when you leave after two days, you will say to yourself: *"If T.J. and Eileen Rohleder Can Make Millions Of Dollars — Then So Can I!"* **YOU'LL BE RIGHT...** because I will show you exactly how we did what we did and how we continue to do what we do!

Am I crazy — TO LET YOU ATTEND
up to 40 OF THESE EVENTS?

My friends said I was crazy if I didn't charge at least **$25,000.00** for the opportunity to let you attend up to 40 of these exclusive wealth-making events... BUT I DON'T CARE. I am glad to let you attend up to 40 of these events... over the next 4 years... to help you go from wherever you are now — to wherever you want to be.

Remember, we plan to hold DOZENS of these 2-day advanced wealth-making Seminars over the next 4 years... **At $3,985.00 each this is a true value of up to $159,400.00!**

But wait, there's still more!

Much, much more!

The NEXT SECTION was written by Chris Lakey, to tell you about THE THIRD PLATINUM MEMBER BENEFIT that you will receive when you join our top-level position!

As you'll see — this is the ULTIMATE WEALTH-MAKING GIFT — that has a real world value of A QUARTER OF A MILLION DOLLARS — and has the power to let you cash in as many as 3 million possible ways!!! *Read on...*

From: Chris Lakey....

PLATINUM MEMBER BENEFIT #3

You Will Also Receive Our Super Valuable Wealth-Making Bonus Gift — <u>Worth</u> <u>Over</u> <u>ONE</u> <u>QUARTER</u> <u>OF</u> <u>A</u> <u>MILLION</u> <u>DOLLARS</u> — For Taking A RISK-FREE Trial Membership

You have the power to make money up to 3 MILLION WAYS! Best of all, everything is done for you! Read on... to see how this ALL NEW Wealth-Making System works.

Hi, Chris again. I'm back with THE MOST AMAZING NEWS — that has the awesome power to make you MORE

MONEY than you have ever seen!

Please read closely... This new wealth system THAT YOU CAN RECEIVE ABSOLUTELY FREE — when you fill your Platinum Membership in the Direct-Response Network — will show you how it's possible to...

Get up each morning — put in 10 minutes of fast and easy work — right from your kitchen table — then take off the rest of the day! Our company and our secret source do everything else for you. Then you get paid as often as every 14 days!

Yes, I'm going to show you how it's potentially possible to sit back and get paid up to three million ways!

Best of all — this is A FREE BONUS to you!

THAT'S RIGHT — you pay ZERO MONEY to receive all three million of these powerful ways to make automatic money!

All 3-MILLION possible ways to make money will be given to you ABSOLUTELY FREE — when you become a Platinum Member of our four year Mentorship Program!

You will receive ALL 3 MILLION POSSIBLE WAYS TO MAKE MONEY — as a totally free gift — just for becoming a Platinum Member!

It's our ULTIMATE FREE WEALTH-MAKING GIFT to you!

Best of all, you hardly do anything to get paid as many as up to three million possible ways!

Does that sound too good to be true?

WELL, IT'S NOT!

My ULTIMATE FREE WEALTH-MAKING GIFT will give you the power to do this! I'll give you a simple formula that you can use to get paid up to three million different ways!

And you don't have to do hardly anything to get this money.

You get up every morning, put in 10 minutes of fast and easy work from your kitchen table, then take the rest of the day off! We do everything else. Then you get paid every 2 weeks for all of the sales that are made for you!

You can live a life that others only dream about:

> Most people work all year. You can potentially make BIG money with this ULTIMATE FREE WEALTH-MAKING GIFT and put in only ten minutes a day!

> Most people get paid by the hour. If they stop working, the money stops coming. But you'll be in position to get paid on the <u>automatic</u> sale of 10,000 of the hottest products on the Internet! Plus, you have 300 proven ways to get paid on these 10,000 red-hot products!

Yes, you'll get 300 ways to get paid on the automatic sale of <u>over</u> 10,000 of the <u>hottest</u> selling products on the Internet! That means you have three million possible ways to get paid huge sums of automatic cash! Best of all, <u>everything</u> is done for you — and you get a check delivered to you every two weeks for all of the automatic sales that are made for you! These commission checks can be sent to you — every 14 days — like clockwork!

With three million possible ways to make money — your friends may think you have won the lottery!

You'll be the talk of the town when you successfully use our ULTIMATE FREE WEALTH-MAKING GIFT! Your friends,

Self-reflection is the school of wisdom.

Baltasar Gracian

The unexamined life is not worth living.

Plato

Life is either a daring adventure or nothing.

Helen Keller

family, and neighbors will all wonder what you're doing to make money. After all, you don't have a job... You don't go to work every day... You live in a nice home... drive a nice car... and you're always going somewhere on vacation! (Tease them by sending them a postcard!)

But don't worry. Nobody has to know what you do. This isn't one of those wealth-making methods you have to drag other people into. Let other people wonder what you're doing to earn your money. And give them a big wink and a smile when you drive by in your shiny new car!

I wish our company could take credit for this breakthrough. We can't. It was discovered by a few other people. — However, we can take credit for getting this into the hands of the people who want to use this discovery to become very rich...

You see, <u>almost</u> everyone who already knows about this amazing discovery is keeping it a secret. Only a couple of these people are talking and they are charging HUNDREDS and even THOUSANDS OF DOLLARS...

More about that later.

Right now, I want to tell you ALL about this amazing breakthrough — and help you COMPLETELY UNDERSTAND the basics of how it works...

<u>To Help You Understand</u> — <u>I Must Start By Giving You</u> A Normal Marketing Example

You must see how you can make money using the standard approach — to understand <u>*WHY*</u> this is the breakthrough it is.

So let's begin at the beginning...

Let's pretend you are a magazine publisher — and you

have a magazine that millions of people want to read. And let's also say that y<u>ou</u> have thousands of products that y<u>ou</u> want to sell in your own magazine. — Now all you have to do is print your magazine — and then distribute it to millions of people who will see your advertisements — and then order your products.

Think of the wealth-making power this would give you!

Can you imagine owning a magazine that was <u>loaded</u> with thousands of your own advertisements that sold your products?

Now let's pretend you published 300 of these magazines that gave tens of millions of people the valuable information they want. All of them would be jam-packed with your ads that sold your products.

But wait. It gets even better!

<u>Now</u> <u>let's</u> <u>continue</u> <u>our</u> <u>example</u>...

Let's also pretend that you had over 10,000 super valuable products that you advertised inside each one of your magazines.

This would give you 300 different magazines that were badly wanted by tens of millions of people. And inside each magazine you would sell over 10,000 in-demand products!

Add it up. You'll see. 300 magazines that each sold over 10,000 products would mean...

You'd have over 3 million possible ways to sit back and get paid huge sums of money!

You would print your 300 magazines and have them distributed on magazine racks across the world. Then all you'd do is wait for all the orders to come flooding to you for the 10,000+

hot products that were sold inside each magazine!

If you were able to pull this off — you would have the kind of wealth-making power that the richest people can only dream of.

But let's take our powerful example two steps further...

First, let's say that the 10,000+ hot products that were sold inside your magazines were all shipped by other people.

Yes, other people took care of all the product development fees — they did all the shipping of the products for you — and they handled all of the customer service headaches and hassles for you!

If this happened, you would be in the powerful position to collect huge sums of automatic money from the sale of these 10,000+ hot products — *without* any of the headaches and hassles that most people are forced to go through! **You would be making money on over 10,000 in-demand products that other people developed for you — and you'd sell them in your 300 valuable magazines that were available on magazine racks around the world.**

Does that sound exciting to you? I certainly hope so.

After all, you would have OVER 3 MILLION WAYS TO MAKE MONEY — *without* shipping a single product!

You would be in the amazing position to sit back and collect money as many as over three million ways with...

✓ **NO** product development costs.

✓ **NO** customer service staff.

✓ **NO** marketing department to develop all the promotional

The mass of men lead lives of quiet desperation.

Henry David Thoreau

Early to bed, early to rise, makes a man healthy, wealthy and wise.

Benjamin Franklin

Work is the ultimate medicine!

T. J. Rohleder

materials to sell the products.

✓ **NO** research and development costs.

✓ **NO** endless hours of all the frustrating headaches and hassles that must be gone through to develop any product.

Consider the wealth-making power you'd enjoy...

You would be making money on over 10,000 super hot products, which were sold inside all 300 of your own magazines — _without_ any of the headaches, hassles, high costs, and endless frustrations it takes to develop and fulfill these products!

Your only cost would be having each magazine written, printed, and distributed for you.

Oh, there's the rub!

Yes, this is where the example ends, right?

After all, it would cost tens and perhaps hundreds of millions of dollars — to print and distribute 300 magazines, wouldn't it?

And yet there are thousands of different magazines being written, printed, and distributed all over the world. Each one can cost millions of dollars just to get it on the newsstand.

And who pays for all of the high cost of printing and distribution?

You're right, it's the...

Advertisers!

Advertisers are more than happy to collectively pay billions of dollars to have their ads placed in these magazines because they <u>know</u> that a percentage of the readers are the kind of people

who... are looking for the items they sell.

You know all of this. But unless you're in the publishing business, you probably don't think twice about it. — All you care about is watching your favorite TV shows or reading your favorite magazines and newspapers... Who cares about the advertisers who help pay for all of it, right?

Well, just for the sake of this example, I want you to think like a magazine publisher. Imagine if you had all of the things we've talked about so far...

> *IF* you were the publisher of 300 valuable magazines that were distributed around the world.

> And *IF* inside each magazine you were able to sell over 10,000 of the hottest products available without any of the headaches and hassles of product development and fulfillment...

You would have over three million ways to make money!

But wait. It gets even better!

Now let's take our hypothetical example one step further...

Let's say you had millions of advertisers who were more than happy to print and distribute your 300 magazines which sold your 10,000+ products. Yes, all 300 of your magazines written, laid out, printed, and then distributed for you... *absolutely FREE!*

IF this were to happen, you could make money over three million ways — with ZERO costs!

You could sit back on your own private island and collect mega-bucks over three million possible ways — with

millions of other people putting up all the money and doing all the work for you!

Can you see all of this?

Can you imagine it for even a moment?

Does this excite you?

Did you wish you could be the person who was able to make money over three million ways — with other people spending their money while you sat back and collected all the money?

Or does this sound like a fantasy to you?

Does this sound like something you can only dream of? Well, I would have said that, too. But that was <u>before</u> I discovered the secrets I am about to share with you! You see...

What I'm about to show you really does have the power to make you huge sums of money — as many as over 3 million possible ways!

As you are about to see, **this really is like owning 300 of your own magazines and then sitting back and getting paid up to three million different ways from the automatic sale of over 10,000 products that other people research, develop, and deliver for you!** And best of all, it is a way that you could potentially have up to millions of advertisers who are more than happy to cover all of the costs!

So now that you've seen my example, let me begin to show you how our ULTIMATE FREE WEALTH-MAKING GIFT is designed to make you money up to 3 million possible ways.

Please read closely. I think you're about to be very impressed...

A plumber was called by a frantic homeowner to stop a leak in the upstairs bathroom. The plumber quickly took stock of the situation, took his hammer, and hit the pipe hard. The leak stopped. The customer was delighted, until she received the bill for $180.35. "This is outrageous," she protested. "All you did was hit the pipe once." By way of response, the plumber itemized the bill: "Wear and tear on hammer, 35 cents. Knowing where to hit, $180.00."

This _is_ a totally new way to stay home and get rich. And we firmly believe that...

"This will create many new millionaires in the next 24 months."

That's _only_ our strong belief, but it's _backed_ up by _solid_ _fact_. **You see, this really is the greatest marketing breakthrough the world has _ever_ seen!**

Here's why:

Our ULTIMATE FREE WEALTH-MAKING GIFT combines 3 of the _hottest_ new wealth-making methods to sweep the Internet!

Each one of these 3 methods is _already_ generating massive sums of...

money! EACH ONE IS ROCK-SOLID. And yes, each one is _already_ making average people big money... *right now!*

Yes, right now — as you are reading my words — there are many people around the world who are already getting paid huge sums of money with all three of these amazing methods!

Each one is very powerful and can make you rich all by itself...

But when you mix all three of these amazing billion-dollar methods together, they create the ultimate wealth-making explosion that has the awesome power to make you more money than most doctors or lawyers can _ever_ dream of making!

When mixed together, these _three_ billion-dollar Internet methods really can **let you stay home and get paid as many as over three million possible ways!** But because it is all so new

---

and somewhat high-tech in nature, I had to give you the real-world example of how it could be possible to make money up to three million ways.

Now let me show you how it all ties together...

Here we go:

The three Internet wealth-makers that are now combined together to let you get paid up to three million ways are:

Internet Wealth-Making Method **#1** — **Electronic Books**

Internet Wealth-Making Method **#2** — **Affiliate Marketing**

Internet Wealth-Making Method **#3** — **Chain-Reaction Marketing**

Each one of these Internet wealth-makers is still fairly new! Yes, if you are a high-tech Internet savvy person, you already know about each one of these Internet wealth-making methods. But they are still new — because the Internet itself is still new!

Think about it: The World-Wide Web (WWW), that opened the Internet up for billions of average people, was only launched in 1993 — and did not start sweeping the globe until several years later.

Because of this...

The Internet is still brand new!

Sure, there are already many Internet millionaires, and even some billionaires, who made their fast fortune in a few years. But many billions of Internet dollars are still out there — just waiting to be made by people like you and me!

So just because you have heard about these three Internet wealth-makers does not mean that you can't get rich with them.

You can. In fact, you can get rich with just <u>one</u> of these amazing breakthroughs.

But when you mix these three Internet wealth-making methods together, they give you <u>even</u> <u>more</u> wealth-making power!

Mixing all three of these <u>proven</u> Internet wealth-makers gives you the awesome power to make your fortune the same basic way I told you about in my example...

As I proved to you, if you could do all of the things we talked about earlier — you would have the power to make money over three million ways — <u>*with extremely low costs!*</u>

As you saw, this would give you the ultimate wealth-making power! **And this example was the perfect way to describe our all-new ULTIMATE FREE WEALTH-MAKING GIFT!**

Here's how:

<u>Internet Wealth-Making Method #1</u> —

The Electronic Books you will receive the Rights to are like having 300 of your own magazines!

<u>Internet Wealth-Making Method #2</u> —

The Affiliate Marketing system I have already set up for you PAYS YOU HUGE PROFITS on over 10,000 hot products! Best of all, other people take care of <u>all</u> the headaches and hassles of the researching, development, and fulfillment costs for you!

These first two wealth-makers are like having 300 of your own magazines that sell over 10,000 of the hottest products for you!

Habit may be likened to a cable; every day we weave a thread, and soon we cannot break it.

You can never be too rich or too thin.

Wallis Warfield Simpson

Advertise, or the sheriff may do it for you.

P. T. Barnum

But the next major wealth-maker lets other people distribute your "magazines" to the millions of people who are <u>perfect</u> candidates to buy your 10,000+ products!

Internet Wealth-Making Method #3 —

Chain Reaction Marketing is the final ingredient that lets other people <u>gladly</u> spend their own time and money to distribute your 300 "magazines" (which are <u>really</u> valuable Electronic Books!) for you!

Chain Reaction Marketing is a powerful new way that Web-Site owners can get absolutely FREE Internet advertising that works!

> They get a powerful and proven way to get more people to visit and re-visit their Web-Sites.

> And you get a proven way to have up to thousands of other people making money for you!

Here's how it works:

1. **You start with some kind of "digital product" that has real value — such as an <u>Electronic</u> <u>Book</u>!** Electronic Books have all the value of a real book you pay for, but they are delivered in a 100% digital format.

2. **You give Web-Site owners permission to give away your Electronic Book — absolutely FREE!** This gives people a great gift just for coming to their Web-Sites. <u>Everyone loves getting a valuable FREE gift</u>! So offering your FREE Electronic Book is a powerful "Ethical Bribe" that gives people a great reason for coming to their Web-Sites! Your FREE Electronic Book now becomes a powerful promotional tool for helping Web-Site owners make more money.

3. **All the people who receive your FREE Electronic Book**

are also <u>strongly</u> <u>encouraged</u> to give it away for free to as many of their friends and associates as possible! And it's so <u>easy</u> for them to do this! In fact, almost all of the people on the Internet pass along Electronic Files to each other all the time. And everyone loves giving and receiving FREE Gifts.

And here's where it really heats up...

Every time they give away your FREE Electronic Book, <u>you</u> and the Web-Site owner can get paid!

How much money can you make? Well, first, let me show you how the Web-Site owners profit:

These Web-Site owners can give away your Electronic Book to just 10 people who each give it away to ten more people, who each do the same! Your Electronic Book could quickly be given away to tens of thousands of people! **And the Web-Site owner's special link <u>THAT</u> <u>MAKES</u> <u>IT</u> <u>EASY</u> <u>FOR</u> <u>PEOPLE</u> <u>TO</u> <u>COME</u> <u>BACK</u> <u>TO</u> <u>THEIR</u> <u>WEB-SITE</u> will <u>still</u> be inside each Electronic Book, no matter how many of them are given away!**

This is the powerful FREE Internet advertising method that millions of Web-Site owners are desperately searching for!

It's a great thing for them. But it's even greater for you!

Why? That's the most SHOCKING PART! You see...

Because you can be in position to make giant sums of money every time these thousands of Electronic Books are given away! The more Electronic Books that are given away by other people, the more money you can make! This is the key to our amazing new System that is designed to make you huge sums of money as many as over three million ways!

Here's how it works:

Inside your Electronic Book is <u>not</u> only the special link for the Web-Site owner who originally gave it away — but also your own special links that sell as many of your own products as possible!

This is such an AMAZING BREAKTHROUGH and it's so easy:

The Web-Site owner offers your FREE Electronic Book to the people who have visited their site in the past. These people are pleased to receive this great FREE gift and now pass it out to all of their closest friends and associates. They, too, are happy to receive this FREE gift and pass it along to as many others as possible. This can set off a huge, never-ending chain reaction! All of your Electronic Books that are given away for FREE contain <u>your</u> <u>links</u> that make people want to go and check out your products. Each time they buy — you get paid!

This is so brilliant! And it really works! So now you're probably wondering...

"So, how do I get paid up to over three million ways?"

Okay, now it's time to tell you about our all-new ULTIMATE FREE WEALTH-MAKING GIFT and show you how all of this works.

Here we go...

As you know, our all-new ULTIMATE FREE WEALTH-MAKING GIFT is a powerful combination of three of the hottest wealth-making breakthroughs the Internet has ever seen.

Here they are again:

1. Electronic Books

2. Affiliate Marketing

3. Chain Reaction Marketing

All 3 of these wealth-makers are part of a long-term trend on the global Internet. Each is <u>already</u> making people super rich <u>right</u> <u>now</u>! And when you mix these 3 wealth-making breakthroughs together, you have even more power to make even more money!

Here's how we have done this for you:

<u>Internet Wealth-Making Breakthrough #1</u> —

We give you the Joint Ownership to 300 of the very best Electronic Books on the Internet!

Each one of these Electronic Books was written on the one subject people will <u>never</u> get enough of: **MAKING MONEY**!

Almost everyone on the Internet wants to make more money — and that's exactly what these 300 powerful Electronic Books tell them how to do! Best of all, when you receive our all-new ULTIMATE FREE WEALTH-MAKING GIFT, you are getting the complete joint owner rights to all 300 of these super valuable Electronic Books that are wanted and needed by tens of millions of people on the world-wide Internet!

But this is only the beginning!

Yes, this <u>is</u> <u>only one</u> of the three Internet wealth-makers that you will receive when you send for our amazing new breakthrough!

It gets even better! Read on...

You will start off with OVER 10,000 of the hottest Affiliate Programs on the Internet! This gives you over 10,000 super exciting ways to make automatic cash on the global Internet! Best of all, brand new and profitable Affiliate Programs will be added daily — at no charge to you! And under-performing products will be removed — guaranteeing that you will always have the Rights to sell the hottest, best-selling products!

And if that's not exciting enough for you, we will take it one giant step further! Our revolutionary ULTIMATE FREE WEALTH-MAKING GIFT really does give you the greatest marketing breakthrough the Internet has ever seen because...

We have combined the first two of these powerful and proven ways to get rich on the Internet!

Here's how: **We have added these over 10,000 highly unique and super profitable Affiliate programs to all 300 of your valuable Electronic Books that you'll get the joint owner rights to!**

Yes, both of these first two Internet wealth-makers have now been added together to create a giant explosion that has the potential power to let you stay home and get paid a total of over three million exciting and proven ways!

It's amazing, but true...

By mixing these first two powerful Internet wealth-making methods together, you now have the awesome

The first quality that is needed [in an artist] is audacity.

Winston Churchill

A professional writer is an amateur who didn't quit.

Richard Bach

To escape criticism — do nothing, say nothing, be nothing.

Elbert Hubbard

power to stay home and make huge sums of money over three million proven and exciting ways!

Go back to the example I gave you earlier. Do you remember the power you would have if you were the publisher of 300 magazines that each sold over 10,000 valuable products that other people researched, developed, and shipped for you?

Well, this is <u>EXACTLY</u> the kind of get-rich power you have with these first two Internet wealth methods that we have mixed together:

> **The 300 Electronic Books we give you really are similar to valuable magazines!** Each one regularly sells for $14.95 each and they're worth it! And you will receive the full Joint Owner rights. **This gives you the same powerful benefits you would receive if you spent the small fortune we spent to develop all 300 of these powerful Electronic Books!** So this really is like being the publisher of 300 valuable magazines that millions of people want!

> **And the over 10,000 Affiliate Programs sell red-hot in-demand products that millions of people on the Internet really want! These products are already selling like crazy!**

So add it up:

Here's how this ULTIMATE FREE WEALTH-MAKING GIFT gives you a total of over 3-million possible ways to get paid:

A. All 300 of the Electronic Books make it super easy for people to find and order <u>one</u> or <u>more</u> of these 10,000+ hot products!

B. We will add a powerful search engine into all 300 of your Electronic Books! This amazing high-tech search engine lets the people who get your Electronic Books simply punch in the subject they are interested in — and up pops the special Affiliate Web-Sites that offer to give them <u>exactly</u> what they are looking for.

C. Then they can quickly order these 10,000+ hot products and you get paid every 14 days!

<u>Nothing</u> could be easier! This gives you the power to make money a combination of up to over 3-million automatic ways!

And if that's <u>still</u> not exciting enough for you... *brace yourself.*

Because now I'm going to show you how we added the final Internet wealth-making method — to make this the greatest marketing breakthrough the world has <u>ever</u> seen.

Internet Wealth-Making Breakthrough #3 —

You are also receiving a total of 300 super-valuable Chain Reaction Marketing Web-Sites that are designed to let as many as tens of thousands of other people on the Internet make money for you!

You will receive 300 of the most powerful Chain Reaction Web-Sites on the Internet!

Each one is designed to let Web-Site owners add their own Web-Site advertisement to all 300 of your Electronic Books — to get people to visit and re-visit their Web-Sites!

They will pass your Electronic Books out to as many people as they possibly can to an ever-growing number of people on the Internet.

Best of all, each time someone receives <u>just one</u> of your

valuable Electronic Books, you can get paid as many as over 10,000 proven ways!

Add it up. You'll see:

Each Electronic Book that is distributed for you has the ability to make you money as many as over 10,000 different ways.

And since you will jointly own 300 of these valuable Electronic Books, you can easily see that this really does give you a grand total of over 3-million proven ways to get paid!

Best of all, by adding this final Internet wealth-maker to the mix, other people will be greatly rewarded to distribute your 300 Electronic Books for you!

So consider everything we have talked about in this letter. We have covered a lot of ground. But when you <u>stop</u> and carefully consider everything we have gone over, you'll see...

This really <u>does</u> give you the awesome ability to make money <u>the same basic way</u> you would in the example I gave you at the start of this section!

I know that making money a total of 3-million possible ways <u>did</u> seem way too good to be true at first. But now you have (hopefully) seen that it is true.

And as I have proven to you, <u>everything</u> in my all-new ULTIMATE FREE WEALTH-MAKING GIFT has been <u>tested</u> and proven to make <u>GIANT</u> sums of money. Each one of the three Internet wealth-making methods that has gone into this amazing get-rich breakthrough is <u>already</u> generating huge sums of money for other people. But mixing them together the way we have done for you gives each one so much <u>more</u> wealth-making power!

So by now, if you have read every word in this section, you are excited and ready to go! In fact, you are probably saying to yourself:

A critic is a man who knows the way but can't drive the car.

Kenneth Tynan

C riticism comes easier than craftsmanship.

Zeuxis, fifth century B.C.

F riendships multiply joys, and divide grief.

Thomas Fuller

"How much does all of this cost?"

I'll tell you how much this costs in a moment — and you will be <u>shocked</u> at the super-low price you will receive by filling out your Application Form and returning it to me <u>before</u> the end of the day.

But first — let me first show you how much all this is worth. After all, there's <u>no way</u> you will ever realize the amazing bargain you are about to receive <u>until</u> and <u>unless</u> you fully understand the true value of everything you're about to receive. So read carefully...

Here Is The Real Value Of All <u>Three</u> Of These Powerful Internet Wealth-Makers That Have Now Been Combined To Make You Rich!

*Here is a **<u>BOLD</u>** but **<u>TRUE</u>** statement:* All <u>three</u> of the Internet wealth-makers you will receive — that have been combined together in a whole new and powerful way — <u>would cost you a small fortune if you tried to hire other people to do it all for you</u>.

I say this with full confidence.

Why?

Because I have spent a small fortune of my own to develop <u>everything</u> that you are about to receive! But don't take my word for it. Do some checking on your own. You'll see that this really would cost you a small fortune <u>if</u> you tried to develop all this on your own.

Here's a quick example of what you would pay to have <u>everything</u> you will receive when you send for our ULTIMATE FREE WEALTH-MAKING GIFT:

Method #1 —

There are thousands of writers who are more than happy to write an Electronic Book for you. Just tell them what you want and they'll go to work right away. Some will even do the research and writing for <u>half</u> the money in advance and the other half when they're done. Finding these writers is easy.

How easy? Well, I once ran a very small ad for a freelance writer in some local newspapers here in Kansas... _I got 74 replies!_

And what will it cost you to hire this writer to write your Electronic Book? The prices vary all over the place. (So does the quality of the writing!) But you can find a good writer to research and create a nice Electronic Book for $10.00 to $20.00 a page.

That's $500.00 to $1,000.00 for each 50 page Electronic Book.

Not a bad price for something that can make you money for the rest of your life!

But, even at this low price, you'd still invest $150,000.00 to $300,000.00 to have 300 Electronic Books written for you.

Sure, you might get a discount if you paid for all 300 at once... But that's <u>only</u> part of your expenses... You also must pay a graphic artist to design a nice cover for you — and do the other layout design work, to make your Electronic Book look nice... and get it Internet ready.   This can easily cost another $200.00 to $400.00 per Electronic Book — bringing your total investment for all 300 Electronic Books to $210,000.00 — to $420,000.00...

THIS IS THE GOSPEL TRUTH!

Investing as much as $420,000.00 for 300 Electronic Books may seem high. **But with the high prices some writers and graphic artists charge, you could pay even more!** Of course, you could pay even less. For example, there are writers, graphic artists, and computer programmers who live in other countries who charge about HALF of this amount. Some do excellent work...

So let's say you track down these talented and very reasonably priced people and hire them. If that would happen, you'd still pay $210,000.00 to have 300 Electronic Books completely done for you. So for the sake of this example, let's use this low figure. Investing $210,000.00 would hurt most people. But it would be a wise investment if you had the money.

Luckily for you, the second Internet wealth-maker would not cost you anywhere near this amount. However, you would pay a high price in another commodity: Time.

Read on....

Method #2 —

It's easy to find 10,000 super-hot Affiliate Programs on the Internet. But it may take you forever to set them up to make automatic money for you!

The Internet is jam-packed with Affiliate Programs! This is good news and bad news.

First, the good news...

Tens of thousands of people have products they want to sell on the Internet. **They are more than happy to pay YOU a generous commission for helping them sell it!** AND THEY MAKE IT SO EASY! All you have to do is learn a few basic high-tech computer skills or hire someone who already knows how to add "Affiliate Links" to your Web-Site. This can take as little as a few minutes to add one of these links to your Web-Site. Then all you do is keep getting people to go to your Web-Site. That's it. **Each new Affiliate Link you add to your Web-Site could make you a steady stream of money that never stops!** The more of

---

Education is a method by which one acquires a higher grade of prejudice.

Laurence J. Peter

Winning isn't everything. It's the only thing.

Vince Lombardi

Use it or lose it.

Freedom lies in being bold.

Robert Frost

these streams you add to your Web-Site, the more money you could easily make! Add enough of these Affiliate Income Streams to your site and you could end up with a raging river of steady cash that pays you a never-ending fortune!

How much will you make?

Nobody can say for sure...

But one woman I know, Rosalind Gardner, says she makes an average of $435,000.00 a year with her Affiliate programs.

Yes, she's making $435,000.00 a year — *without* shipping anything!

That's more than many doctors and lawyers make!

So that's the good news! After all, anything that has the potential of making you $435,000.00 — *without* shipping a single product — is great!

And if you set up all of these Affiliates yourself, it won't cost you anything but the time you spend to do it. So for this reason, I will not place a dollar value on this second Internet wealth-maker. **Although, it could easily cost you thousands of dollars to pay someone to set up all of these Affiliate Programs for you.**

Now for the bad news...

Finding the right Affiliate Programs can take you forever. Plus, you also have the major problem of finding a way to get people to go to your Web-Site and actually see and buy all of the special Affiliate products your Web-Site sells.

This is a huge problem.

Fortunately for you, there IS a golden solution!

And this solution comes from combining the final two Internet Wealth-Makers that will be yours when you let us give you our ULTIMATE FREE WEALTH-MAKING GIFT:

You see, now you receive over 10,000 of the hottest Affiliate Programs — that will be set up in your name — so 100% of the commission comes straight to you! PLUS, you will also receive the most incredible way to get people to find and order these 10,000 products — so you can automatically get paid right away.

Read on...

You'll be VERY IMPRESSED to see how all this is put together for you — and designed to make you a fortune!

Method #3 —

Remember, each Electronic Book that others pass out for you has the ability to pay you up to 10,000+ ways. And because your Chain Reaction Marketing Web-Sites do it all for you — and because you have 300 complete Web-Sites that make it easy to let people pass out all 300 of your valuable Electronic Books — you really do have the power to make money up to 3-million ways!

So how much would it cost to put together a Web-Site that had the Chain Reaction Marketing technology built into it?

That's a great question.

Again, the answer may shock you. You see, it can cost huge sums of money to build a Web-Site that does all this for you.

How much money? JUST LOOK:

Here's The Amount Of Money You'd Pay To Have Someone Build A Web-Site With The Chain-Reaction Marketing Technology:

First, you must find a Web-Site developer who even understands Chain Reaction Marketing. That might be hard. **But if you searched far enough — you could find somebody to do this for you.** After all, there are so many different Web-Site developers on the Internet. And the prices they charge fall all over the place.

But it's safe to say that you can find a Web-Site developer to do a great job for you for well under $1,500.00... maybe less. In fact, you can go on the Internet and find some very good Web-Site developers from other nations such as India who will do a great job for a very reasonable fee...

So, for the sake of this example, let's say you <u>only</u> paid as little as $500.00 to have each one of these Chain Reaction Marketing Web-Sites built for you:

✓ Each one would contain your valuable Electronic Book that would be given away for FREE.

✓ Each one would make it easy for Web-Site owners to automatically add their small advertisement in each one of your 300 Electronic Books.

✓ And each one would also make it super easy for other people to pass out your Electronic Books to others.

If you only paid $500.00 per Web-Site to a good developer who could do all of this for you, it would be a <u>great</u> bargain. But again, that would come to another investment of $150,000.00.

So add it up. You'll see. Each Electronic Book and the Chain Reaction Web-Sites that let others give it away — and puts you in the position to get paid over 10,000 ways could easily cost you $1,000.00 — to $2,000.00, or much, much more. **Of course, you could find a team of writers, graphic artists, computer programmers, and Web-Site developers who would take on the whole job for you — including setting up all of the Affiliate Programs for you — for less than $300,000.00 to $600,000.00...** Again, the prices for all of this highly specialized type of work fall all over the place...

But regardless of whether you spend $600,000.00 — or even $300,000.00 — or even half of that amount, it's still going to cost you a small fortune to have all of this built for you! But now you won't invest anywhere near this amount...

You see, we have combined ALL THREE of these powerful Internet wealth-makers into our ULTIMATE FREE WEALTH-MAKING GIFT and it really is yours absolutely FREE!

It's amazing — *but true:* You won't invest $250,000.00 or more... Or $125,000.00... Or $50,000.00... Or even $10,000.00... Heck, you won't even pay $5,000.00... Or even $3,000.00...

No! Because right now — by taking action today:

#1: You'll get the Joint Owner Rights to all 300 Electronic Books.

#2: Plus, all 10,000+ of the powerful Affiliate Programs will be set up in your name — so all the money comes straight to you as often as every 14 days.

#3: Plus, you'll receive the 300 complete Chain Reaction Marketing Web-Sites that make it easy for up to thousands of other people to pass out your FREE Electronic Books to everyone they know.

And you can get ALL THIS, starting today...

ABSOLUTELY FREE!!!

That's right. For a limited time we will set you up with all 300 Electronic Books and all 10,000+ Affiliate Programs and all 300 Chain Reaction Marketing Web-Sites — ABSOLUTELY FREE — when you join us as a Platinum-Level Member of our Direct-Response Network.

Just go ahead and fill out the Platinum Member Application Form by going to the website at the bottom of every other page in this book — and RUSH it back to our office today. Do this RIGHT NOW and we'll make sure you get this ULTIMATE FREE WEALTH-MAKING GIFT that is designed to make you automatic cash — as many as up to 3 million powerful ways!

But that's not all! NO WAY. NOT BY A LONG SHOT! There are still two more Platinum Member Benefits you'll love! So please read on... Now I'll turn it back over to T.J. and let him tell you all about the next amazing way your Platinum Membership is designed to help you get rich! Read closely. I think you'll be very impressed, to put it mildly...

Times of general calamity and confusion produce great minds. The purest ore is produced from the hottest furnace, and the brightest thunderbolt is elicited from the darkest storms.

Charles Caleb Colton

With ever disadvantage, there is always a greater advantage.

W. Clement Stone

Another Exciting Message From T.J. Rohleder....

PLATINUM MEMBER BENEFIT #4

This Section tells you about THE GREATEST MEMBER BENEFIT you'll get when you become a Platinum Member. *Read on, as I show you:*

"How To Get Paid $2,000.00 Cash For Mailing One Yellow Flier!"

✓ **We close all of the sales for you!** We talk to the people who get your Magic Yellow Flier — Answer their questions — and then close all of the big-ticket sales for you!

✓ **We immediately write you a big fat check for $2,000.00 for each and every sale we make for you!** Then we put your commission check(s) in a Fed-ex envelope and have Federal Express deliver them to you the next day! **You take your $2,000.00 checks to the bank and cash them!**

Then you can take the rest of the day off!

✓ **Best of all, the same experts who help us make millions each year can print and mail all the Magic Yellow fliers for you!**

✓ Read on to see how this powerful Platinum Member Benefit #4 is designed to make you rich!

HELLO AGAIN,

T.J. Rohleder here, to tell you about THE GREATEST MEMBER BENEFIT that you will receive when you become a Platinum Member. Please read closely. Be prepared to be shocked!

If you carefully read my headline above, you know:

This fourth Platinum Member Benefit is a simple and easy way you can get paid $2,000.00 cash for each and every Platinum Membership sale we close for you! Our System does it all for you! All you do is mail the yellow flier and collect the cash!

This is a win/win situation for you and me:

YOU WIN BECAUSE — all you do is mail out the Magic Yellow Flier or let our experts do this for you. Then you get a check for $2,000.00 cash for every sale we close for you! **Plus, you will also be in the powerful position to receive A 100% MATCHING BONUS on any and all of the monthly income we pay to these people.** This gives you the potential power to get paid huge sums of EXTRA automatic income for doing virtually nothing!

AND WE WIN BECAUSE — you will be letting us focus all our time and energy into making the largest number of these high level Membership sales to the people who get your flier.

This is a great partnership between BOTH of us:

You will be playing a part in helping us and we will do our part by making all the sales for you and rushing you a FAT check for a whopping $2,000.00 for each sale we close for you!

It is in our best interest to make the largest number of Platinum Membership sales to the people who get your yellow flier. After all, the more money we make for you, the more we make too!

But that's not all. You see, THE PEOPLE WHO RECEIVE YOUR FLIER ALSO WIN! These people WIN BIG — by getting the chance to make huge sums of money by becoming a Platinum Member of our Direct-Response Network.

The more you know about this, the more excited you'll be! Please read closely. I have so much to tell you. *But I must start by giving you some...*

> Good news...

> Bad news...

> AND MORE GOOD NEWS!

Please read closely. What I have to say to you has the potential power to make you super rich! *Here we go...*

✓ *First, the Good News:* This is a proven money-making system that is based on the same methods that have already me millions of dollars.

Yes, my One Magic Flier Miracle is a complete system that is proven in every way. This is real. It is ROCK-SOLID. And, best of all, it is based on a proven wealth-making system that has already brought in many millions of dollars.

Will you make millions of dollars with this system?

I honestly don't know. And I'm not promising that you will. But the potential for you to make a fortune is definitely here!

One thing is certain: You will get a check for $2,000.00 cash for every Platinum Membership sale we close for you. Plus, you will also receive A 100% MATCHING BONUS on any and all of the monthly income we pay to these people!

Listen closely. I cannot guarantee that you will make millions of dollars or <u>any</u> specific sum of money with my One Magic Flier Miracle System. Do you understand this? Good. But I can promise you that this easy-to-use system is based on the same methods that have brought me many millions of dollars.

That's the good news!

Why? Because I firmly believe that...

The same methods that have made someone else many millions of dollars can also make <u>YOU</u> a huge fortune.

Making huge sums of money is a lot like a cake recipe, if you follow the instructions to a "t" — you can bake a great cake. Making money is like this, too. **Just find out <u>exactly</u> how someone else is making their own fortune. Then duplicate their exact methods. When you do this the right way, you can make a fortune, too!**

<u>NEVER</u> <u>FORGET</u> <u>THIS</u>:

The same multi-million dollar systems that provide a huge fortune for one person can be 100% duplicatable. Remember this simple wealth-making rule and you <u>can</u> use it to get very rich!

<u>And</u> <u>that</u> <u>brings</u> <u>me</u> <u>to</u> <u>a</u> <u>major</u> <u>problem</u>...

Many of the money-making programs are worthless garbage

that have <u>never</u> been proven to make anyone any money — except the promoters who sell them to people like you and me.

This is sad, but true. Most of the money-making plans that promise to help you get rich are worthless. Someone came up with an idea that "sounded good" and now they want to make their fortune by trying to sell it to millions of people like you and me. <u>The people who promote these plans are liars and cheaters</u>. They make <u>all</u> their money selling their "plans," "programs," and "systems." They don't give a damn if the people who buy these systems make <u>any</u> money or not.

OUR RAGS-TO-RICHES STORY...

If you're like me, you have been lied to and cheated many times on your quest for a true money-making system that really works. Is this true? **IF SO, WE HAVE MUCH IN COMMON.** You see, for years my wife, Eileen, and I sent away for one money-making plan after another — <u>only to be disappointed</u>. We were lied to more times than we could count by people who promised to give us a simple plan we could use to make a lot of money.

We blamed ourselves for our lack of success, when it wasn't our fault at all. The fact is, we were using plans and programs that only "sounded good" but <u>never</u> made any money for anyone except the promoters themselves. We thought about quitting many times, but we hung in there. We kept searching. And our faith was rewarded! Finally, we discovered two different money-making plans that were a cut above (from reputable people who actually made their biggest profits by collecting a piece of our profit). And when we mixed these two programs together, we made...

Over $10-million dollars in 4 years.

Yes, we became instant millionaires in a few short years because we finally stumbled onto a couple of plans that were actually producing huge sums of money for other people...

Man is still the most extraordinary computer of all.

John F. Kennedy

Nothing happens until something is sold.

Arthur H. (Red) Motley

Never look back unless you are planning to go that way.

The same thing could happen to you! All you need is a proven money-making system that really works! And this is exactly what you are getting with our One Magic Page Flier System that is yours when you become a Platinum Member!

As you'll see, we have taken the best-of-the-best of the secrets that have made us many tens of millions of dollars and put them into a very complete and easy system for you! Best of all, our success is <u>directly</u> tied to your success. What do I mean by that? And <u>why</u> is this so important? Simple: *WE MAKE OUR BIGGEST PROFIT BY COLLECTING A SMALL PERCENTAGE OF EVERY DOLLAR WE PUT IN YOUR POCKET.* In fact, the more money we can help <u>you</u> make, the more <u>we</u> make too. So it really is in our best interest to help you make the largest amount of money with our One Magic Flier System that will be yours when you become a Platinum Member.

As you will see, this powerful system has been proven to generate millions of dollars. It is 100% complete and ready to go! Just mail the One Magic Flier or let others mail it for you. That's it. This is so easy a 12-year-old child can do it! We take it from there and do our best to close as many sales as possible to the people who get your Magic Yellow Flier in the mail.

The more sales we can make for <u>you</u>, the more money we put in our own pocket. That's <u>why</u> it is in our most selfish interests to make as many sales as we possibly can and then Federal Express your checks for $<u>2,000.00</u> for each Platinum Membership sale we close for you! All you do is mail the fliers and wait for the Federal Express driver to show up with your checks! Nothing could be simpler! Nothing is easier. And this <u>is</u> a true partnership where <u>BOTH</u> of us have the power to make giant sums of money!

However, there is one more problem... Thank goodness it's a problem that is fast and easy to solve. But it is still a major situation you <u>must</u> know about.

That brings us to...

✔ ***The Bad News:*** **You must be a Platinum-Level Distributor for the Direct-Response Network to get paid $2,000.00 CASH for each Platinum Membership sale we close for you.**

As you know, the Direct-Response Network is a proven way to get rich in Multi-Level Marketing without talking to a single person...

This is a new wealth-making opportunity that mixes Multi-Level Marketing with the full power of Mail Order Marketing and four other multi-billion dollar methods. *THE RESULT:* A complete system that is designed to make average people super rich in Multi-Level Marketing <u>without</u> talking to a single person or doing any personal selling!

The D.R.N. is designed to give you the easy-to-use turn-key system you need to get rich from home! We have taken the best-of-the-best of the secrets we have discovered since 1988 to generate over $100-million dollars in sales and put them into this amazing MLM opportunity.

This One Magic Flier Wealth System is <u>just</u> <u>one</u> of the turn-key systems we have developed to let our Distributors make huge sums of money.

But only Platinum Level Distributors will get paid $2,000.00 CASH on every sale we close.

HERE'S WHY:

➤ We had to give our Platinum Members the BIGGEST REWARD for joining this top-level Membership... and letting you keep $<u>2,000.00</u> on every sale we close for you is it!

➤ Our Platinum Level Distributors deserve the opportunity to make the largest amount of money — right out of the gate... *and this is it!*

So the bad news is the simple fact that the opportunity to get a check for $2,000.00 cash for every Platinum Membership sale we close for you — then receive A 100% MATCHING BONUS on any and all of the monthly income we pay to these people — is only available to our Platinum Members.

<u>But this does not have to be bad news for you!</u>

In fact, that brings me to...

✓ MORE GOOD NEWS that may be the <u>best</u> money-making news... *ever!*

Here's what it's all about...

THE BEST NEWS: **Now you can become a Platinum Member and get a top Platinum Level Distributor position in the Direct-Response Network!** We believe this opportunity will take the world by storm and make many people multi-millionaires! This is only our prediction and opinion and not a guarantee or promise that you "<u>will</u>" make millions of dollars. But the more you know about this new opportunity, the more you'll see that the powerful potential to make a fortune is here!

Best of all,

When you become a Platinum Member — you will receive our One Magic Flier Wealth System that lets you get paid $2,000 CASH for every sale we close for you!

Yes, it's true! This One Magic Flier Wealth System that lets you get paid a whopping $2,000.00 CASH on every sale we make for you — is only available to my Platinum Members who join now.

That's the ultimate good news I have for you!

In fact, as you'll see, these top-level Members will also receive a top Distributor position in the Direct-Response Network. As you'll see, this could be worth a huge fortune to you!

We have discovered a new way to tap into a multi-billion dollar market that other MLM companies are hardly touching. Because of this, **we firmly believe that there are hundreds of millions of dollars just sitting on the table — waiting to be made. And <u>you</u> can get your fair share of it!**

Now here's the rub:

Our Magic Yellow Flier is just one of the simple, but amazingly powerful ways we are going after the hundreds of millions of dollars that are up for grabs!

Here is the multi-billion dollar market that no MLM company is successfully reaching:

Tens of millions of people who want to stay home and make more money <u>without</u> all the headaches and hassles of a normal business.

Our research has proven to us that <u>this</u> is a multi-billion dollar market that is virtually untapped!

Consider this: A recent survey reported that over 70% of all the people reported that they did <u>not</u> like their job and secretly wished they could find something else. These people had too many financial obligations to give up their current jobs. And yet, they went to work each day to a job they did <u>not</u> enjoy.

Our research has also proven to us that tens of millions of

people secretly dream of starting their own business, but they DON'T want all the headaches and hassles of a regular business...

Please consider what I have just told you and you'll agree:

There may be up to 100-million people who would <u>love</u> to stay home and make huge sums of money — <u>without</u> all of the headaches and hassles of a normal business... and our new MLM company is the answer they're searching for!

Of course, nobody knows what the "real" number is. But you cannot argue with the fact that there is a huge market out there of people who desperately want all of the greatest things that a thriving business can give them — <u>without</u> having to suffer through all the headaches and hassles. This is just <u>one</u> of the enormous markets we are tapping into with our revolutionary new Multi-Level Marketing company! Nobody can say for sure how much money anyone will make, but we <u>firmly</u> <u>believe</u>

There are hundreds of millions of dollars on the table... just waiting to be made. And our Magic Yellow Flier is just <u>one</u> of the secret weapons we are using to help you get this enormous wealth!

This is the fastest money you'll ever make money in your life — bar none!

Here are the 7 simple and easy steps that are designed to make a fortune for you:

STEP #1 — Sign up as a Platinum Member of our D.R.N.. We will RUSH you a special FAST-START PACKAGE that makes it easy for you to start getting paid up to $2,000.00 cash for just one Magic Yellow Flier you drop in the mail. You can order these custom-printed fliers directly from our printer...

Whatever you want to do, do it now. There are only so many tomorrows.

Michael Landon

Action is the antidote to despair.

Joan Baez, Folksinger

You can't cross the sea merely by staring at the water.

Rabindranath Tagore

Then mail out these turn-key fliers or postcards with your referral ID # printed on it. (We supply these fliers to you and can even have them put in the mail for you!)

STEP #2 — The people who get your flier call us. We take it from there and have our professionally trained salespeople tell them all about the five powerful wealth-making benefits they can receive when they become a Platinum-Level Member. Our sales reps will do their very best to sell these top-level Memberships for you!

STEP #3 — Our sales team gets paid hundreds of dollars for each of these high-level Membership sales we make for you — so we are more than happy to make all the sales we can to the people who get your flier and call us!

STEP #4 — **You get paid $2,000.00 cash for each sale we close!**

STEP #5 — Your check for $2,000.00 is *RUSHED* to you as often as EVERY DAY, Monday through Friday — by Federal Express!

STEP #6 — You wait for the Federal Express van to show up — cash your $2,000.00 checks — and then mail more of the fliers we send to you!

This Is The Ultimate Money-Making Partnership!

You do your part by mailing these fliers or postcards. We take it from there. We do all the selling for you! Then we send you BIG FAT CHECKS for a whopping $2,000.00 — for each sale we close! **Nothing is easier!** Plus, we take care of all the customer service work for you, product fulfillment, and all the other headaches and hassles. It's so simple. You can even let our expert suppliers print and mail the postcards or fliers for you!

And to top it off...

STEP #7 — You can also be in the position to get paid even more cash — after we make each sale for you and then pay you the checks for $2,000.00! **As you'll see, this is the icing on your get-rich cake!** It's money that can keep coming to you for doing absolutely nothing! We'll tell you how this works when you sign up and join us!

This is so simple and easy! Best of all, you really will receive this complete Magic Flier Wealth System — and all of the other easy-to-use marketing systems we will develop in the future — when you become a Platinum-Level Member of our revolutionary company!

This amazing new Magic Flier Wealth System has the power to pay you GIANT sums of upfront cash — then pay you a huge monthly income that keeps growing BIGGER without you doing anything!

THIS BEATS EVERY OTHER HOME-BASED BUSINESS OPPORTUNITY.

With most opportunities, the money STOPS if you stop. This means you <u>NEVER</u> get a break. You are constantly forced to work hard or the money will dry up fast. You become a slave to your business and become burned out fast. After a while you just can't take it anymore and finally give up on your dream of financial independence.

<u>The Platinum Member Benefit #4 Solution</u>:

This amazing wealth-making opportunity gives you the <u>TWO</u> <u>TYPES</u> OF MONEY YOU NEED TO GET RICH:

#1: Big sums of upfront cash! You get paid $2,000.00 cash

---

on every big-ticket Membership sale that my highly trained sales team closes for you! We close every single sale for you. You will never talk with a single person! Just do your small part and we take it from there and do everything possible to close as many sales as possible and send you big checks for $2,000.00 cash for each sale. These checks are sent to you by overnight mail or Federal Express as often as every day!

#2: ***Huge sums of monthly "residual" income that can keep getting bigger — and never stop coming to you!*** This is amazing, but true! Our system contains powerful wealth-making leverage features that continue paying you huge sums of money — even if you do absolutely nothing! The money can keep coming to you and never stop!

So there you have it. As you have seen, these four powerful Platinum Member Benefits give you the awesome power to stay home each day and make huge sums of money for many years! In fact, as I will prove to you, due to powerful economic and demographic shifts, the very best wealth-making years are still ahead! I will prove to you there are major shifts that are taking place — RIGHT NOW — that give you the power to make huge sums of money with this new Direct Response Network opportunity for the next 10... 20... and even 30 years and beyond! The more you know about all this, the more shocked you'll be!

So if you like everything I have said so far, then you must get all of the secrets behind this revolutionary new wealth-making breakthrough!

And that brings me to the final Member Benefit we have for you...

Good advice; if people don't listen, let adversity teach them.

Ethiopian saying

Never retire. Michelangelo was carving the Rondanini just before he died at 89. Verdi finished his opera Falstaff at 80. And the 80-year-old Spanish artist Goya scrawled on a drawing, "I am still learning."

Dr. W. Gifford-Jones

How Our New "President's Club" Can Make You Set For Life!

This final Platinum Member Benefit can make you more money than all the others combined! In fact, this could potentially be worth millions of dollars to <u>YOU</u>... just like it has been for us.

The above headline is true! Our new "President's Club" is designed to let you sit back and be financially set for life! This final section shows you how.

As you'll see, we saved the best for last! Please read closely...

This final Platinum Member Benefit really could make you more money than the other 4 benefits combined because, with it...

You Will <u>ALWAYS</u> Be Among The First To Join Us And Cash-In With Every New Wealth-Making Breakthrough We Discover! As you'll see, this gives you the same power that is

---

enjoyed by the world's richest people!

Yes, it's amazing, but true! In fact, being among the first to cash-in is the #1 secret of the world's richest people — and now it will be...

Your Ultimate Wealth-Making Secret!

So let me begin this Section by asking you a serious question...

Have you ever wondered why the rich get richer and the poor get poorer?

I have. In fact, I used to ask myself this question over and over again... And each time, I would get so angry... The thought that the rich people were making all the easy money, while we struggled for every dollar, made me so mad that I couldn't drive through a nice neighborhood without being seized with envy...

I would ask myself:

"Why should these people be blessed with fine homes and cars and have all the freedom that an abundance that money can bring — while we can barely pay our bills and keep a roof over our heads."

I was so angry and jealous... But the great thing about our free nation is that...

This country is filled with rich people who used to be dirt poor.

This is what happened to me and my wife... After struggling for years to find a way to make money, we finally discovered a few wealth-making secrets and brought in millions of dollars in a few short years... We began to discover the secret to getting super rich...

This wealth secret was first given to us by our dear friend, Russ von Hoelscher.

Perhaps you're familiar with Russ. He has been a world-class marketer for over 30 years and he's helped more people make more money than anyone we personally know...

When we met Russ in 1989, we were just getting started with our mail-order business and bringing in about $16,000 a month. That was more money than we had ever made and we were filled with joy!

All the bills were getting paid and we were finally able to enjoy life the way the wealthy enjoyed life. Little did we know that we had just barely scratched the surface of what was possible.

Then we met Russ von Hoelscher...

Russ saw one of our ads we were running and contacted us about working with him. He assured us that he had the secrets we needed to take our business to the next level.

Soon our $16,000.00 a month shot through the roof! Suddenly, we were making more than $16,000.00 in one day! Yes, with Russ's help and within no time, we were bringing in as much as $100,000.00 a week.

To make a long story short, with the secrets Russ gave us, we brought in over $10-Million Dollars in less than 5 years!

So what did Russ do for us that made us over ten million dollars in a handful of years?

That's a great question.

The answer can make you rich.

Here it is...

I'm not inspired by what people say. I'm inspired by what I do.

Evander Holyfield

SUCCESS IS SIMPLE: Mario Cuomo, former governor of New York, says his mother once told him: "There's only two rules for being successful. One, figure out exactly what you want to do, and two, do it."

Even if money did grow on trees, most people wouldn't shake a limb to get it.

Al Spong

Russ gave us the same 4 things you will now receive in the new President's Club...

Here are the 4 ways Russ helped us make millions of dollars:

> *The 1st Way Russ Helped Us Get Rich:* Russ introduced us to the most important private contacts and secret sources that he had been doing business with. We continue to use many of these same contacts and sources today — many years after Russ first revealed them to us in the late 1980's...

> *The 2nd Way Russ Helped Us Get Rich:* Russ privately helped us find exciting new ideas and profitable new areas to get into that we would have never discovered without him. These new ideas — and the ability to continue to research and cash-in with even newer ideas — catapulted us from 'thousandaires' to multi-millionaires!

> *The 3rd Way Russ Helped Us Get Rich:* Russ gave us the best-of-the-best of all of his knowledge, experience, and most jealously-guarded million-dollar secrets that he had acquired over the years. Without all this, we would have never brought in tens of millions of dollars.

> *The 4th Way Russ Helped Us Get Rich:* Russ kept us informed of all the exciting new wealth-making breakthroughs — and helped us become among the first people to cash-in with them before anyone else. You'll hear me say it over and over again, **being among the first to get involved with a new emerging trend or technology is one of the fastest ways to make huge amounts of cash!**

These four things have made us many tens of millions of dollar over the years... and they can be worth a fortune to you, too!

Yes, the fact that these are the ways that Russ von Hoelscher made us millions of dollars is all the proof I need to boldly proclaim that they can make you many millions of dollars, too! This is not a promise or guarantee that you will make millions of dollars or any specific sum of money — **but having these same secrets working for you every day can be worth a huge and growing fortune to you and your family.** The more you know about the power of these proven ways that Russ helped us get rich, the more you will realize...

This Is The Amazing Secret Of Why The Rich Get Richer! And Now It Can Be Your Golden Secret To Getting All The Money You Want!

As you'll see — this final Platinum Member benefit really is the icing on your get-rich cake that you can use (along with the other 4 Platinum Member benefits) to become financially independent for life!

Here's how your Membership in our new President's Club is designed to give you the "secret of the rich" that has and is bringing us and many other people millions of dollars:

The 1st Way We Help YOU Get Rich:

We will introduce you to all of our closest secret contact sources and private contacts, just like Russ did for us.

You will get the very best-of-the-best of the same secret sources and private contacts that we have used to make our fortune. All of this wealth-making power will now be yours! We will be your "go between" and give you the formal introduction you need to the same people we use to bring in many millions of dollars. Now these can be your private sources that can help you get rich!

If this were all you were getting with your President's Club Membership, it would be more than enough to make you set for life...

But we're just getting started! *Read on...*

> *The 2nd Way We Help YOU Get Rich:*

We'll do our best to help you make huge sums of extra money in new ways that you would have *NEVER* discovered on your own.

This second method could be worth a fortune to you, just like it has been to us. Why? **Because rich people helping other rich people to find new ways to make more money is the real secret that the wealthiest people use to keep getting richer.** (*Whew, that was a mouthful — BUT IT'S THE GOSPEL TRUTH!*)

Now you will enjoy this same type of power.

We will give you the answers you need to make huge sums of money that you would have never discovered on your own. Remember, this is one of the best ways Russ von Hoelscher helped us make millions of dollars. It has the power to make a huge fortune for you, too!

> *The 3rd Way We Help YOU Get Rich:*

We will be available to you whenever you need us.

We'll give you our valuable knowledge and experience that we have discovered on our own road to wealth. This can be an enormous shortcut to the wealth that you seek!

When people ask us what Russ von Hoelscher did to help us

To stand still is to fall behind.

Don't wish it were easier, wish you were better.

Jim Rohn

Great minds have purposes, others have wishes. Little minds are tamed and subdued by misfortunes; but great minds rise above them.

Washington Irving

quickly become millionaires, we always respond by saying, *"Russ gave us the best of his 20 years of accumulated knowledge and experience."* **Now we'll give you this same wealth-making advantage.** Yes, our ultimate multi-million-dollar secrets and experience will now become YOUR ultimate secrets to making all the money you want, need, and deserve.

And if all this is not exciting enough, the final item on our list can easily be worth a fortune to you...

> *The 4th Way We Help You Get Rich:*

You will be among the first to join us and cash-in with the newest and most exciting wealth-making secrets that we discover!

We are constantly searching for *"THE NEXT BIG THING"* — and when we find it, you'll be among the first to cash-in with it. Please listen closely:

One of the main reasons the rich get richer is because they help each other spot the newest and most powerful wealth-making secrets and then help each other cash-in — before everyone else finds out about them... Whenever a new wealth-making trend emerges, they are always among the first to profit from it. Then they do all they can to help each other make the largest amount of money. **By the time the rest of the world finds out about this new way to make money, it's too late. All of the easy money is gone...**

But this will NEVER happen to you! Because...

Now you can become our special partner, and be among the first to cash-in with us!

Our mentor, Russ von Hoelscher, calls being one of the first

---

to cash-in with an all new wealth-making discovery...

"Picking The Low-Hanging Fruit!"

Russ tells this story:

"If you're smart, you'll walk around and pick as much of the low-hanging fruit before everyone else realizes it is ripe. Once the low-hanging fruit is gone, other people must come in with ladders and other expensive equipment to pick the higher fruit. But all you had to do was grab the low-hanging fruit that was easily within your grasp. THE SAME THING IS TRUE WHEN IT COMES TO GETTING WEALTHY. You must get in before everyone else and be among the first to quickly get the easy money that can be made in the very beginning. Sure, there's usually a lot of money to be made later, but like that high-hanging fruit, you're gonna spend more time, energy, and money to get it."

RUSS IS RIGHT!! **He has helped us make a fortune over the years by being among the first to cash-in on new and exciting trends before the rest of the world found out about them.** For example, with Russ's help, and the help of a few other rich friends, we were among the first to cash-in on the Internet back in the early 1990s. This one trend alone made us millions of dollars in a few short years. And that's just one fast example. There are many more...

The bottom line: Being one of the first to cash-in on a new emerging trend can be worth a larger fortune to you than anything else... And now, when you become a Platinum-Level Member, you will also be a Member of the President's Club. This is our exclusive Club that lets you be among the first to cash-in with these new trends.

The President's Club puts you in position to join us whenever we discover 'THE NEXT BIG THING' that we are convinced will make many people millions of dollars! *IN FACT*...

You Will Become One Of Our Joint Venture Partners And Be In Position To Possibly Make Millions With Us!

Not only will the President's Club put you in position to profit with new trends and technologies... You will also be invited to join our other rich friends and become one of our Joint Venture Partners. **This can give you a valuable head start over all the others who will get in later — and lets you benefit from the close friendships and trust that we have developed among our group of private contacts and secret sources.** Together, we can work closely with you to do our best to help you (and ourselves) get very rich!

Just to be clear: This is not some run-of-the-mill Distributor or Affiliate position. You will be a Joint Venture Partner — and enjoy the same benefits usually only reserved for our close friends and business associates!

So there you have it! As you can see, I really have saved the best for last! And this final Platinum Member Benefit really can make you more money than all the other benefits combined! In fact, this could potentially be worth millions of dollars to you, just like it has been for us.

THE BOTTOM LINE: We are always on the lookout for people who are the most serious about getting rich. **Your positive action of joining our Platinum Membership will prove to us how serious you are about making huge sums of money.** Now, we will be more than happy to provide all five of these powerful Membership Benefits to you.

So, with all this said, please fill your Platinum-Level Membership today!

I have done my best to prove to you that this Platinum Membership gives you all the powerful tools and resources that

In my practice as a psychiatrist, I have found that helping people to develop personal goals has proven to be the most effective way to help them cope with problems. Observing the lives of people who have mastered adversity, I have noted that they have established goals and sought with all their effort to achieve them. From the moment they decided to concentrate all their energies on a specific objective, they began to surmount the most difficult odds.

Ari Kiev

you need to make all the money you want, need, and truly deserve.

Please fill out your enclosed Application (or go to www.BecomeAPlatinumMember.com) and mail or FAX it to us at once!

Do this today and ALL FIVE of these powerful Platinum Member Benefits will be yours!

So now it's time to start wrapping this up...

Here is a small summary to remind you of what you will be receiving...

PLATINUM MEMBER BENEFIT #1:

You will receive our $100-Million Dollar Coaching Program that lets us personally and privately help you cash-in with the same 26 wealth-making secrets that have brought us a total of over $100-Million Dollars in our first 19 years.

You will have private access to us as we personally guide you through our amazing 26 wealth-making methods. This is the most powerful and personal way we can help support and guide you through the same simple-to-understand and easy-to-use *"A-to-Z Wealth-Making Formula"* that we have used to generate tens of millions of dollars worth of direct marketing sales.

But that's not all!

You will also get personal, private access to a small group of the most talented Direct-Response Marketers we know. These are some of the greatest millionaire-making experts on the planet. Each expert is well-grounded in our 26 wealth-making methods. They will be on call — along with us — to help you make your own fortune with these amazing secrets.

If this one Platinum Member Benefit was the only one you were getting, it would be more than worth the cost to join us now. But wait, there's so much more! *In fact, we're just getting started...*

PLATINUM MEMBER BENEFIT #2:

You will attend as many as 40 of our private, wealth-building Workshops that are designed to make you a huge and never-ending fortune.

Each of these powerful Workshops can be life-changing for you. In fact, just one idea you can gain from just one of these Workshops has the potential to make you hundreds of thousands or perhaps millions of dollars. You can attend up to 40 of these Workshops.

Our friend and mentor, Russ von Hoelscher, has a famous quote...

"Just one idea can make you a million dollars!"

Russ is right! We have walked away from past Seminars and Workshops with just one idea that has brought us over a million dollars. And the same thing can happen to you. The purpose of each of our special '$100-MILLION DOLLAR WORKSHOPS' is to help you get rich with the same tips, tricks, and strategies we've used to make over one hundred million dollars in Direct-Response Marketing.

Assuming you actively participate and let us help you, you will walk away from these Workshops a changed person! A new feeling of excitement will take over as you begin to understand these wealth secrets and discover how to let them make you the fortune you seek!

Our powerful Workshops and Seminars have sold for as much as $4,985.00 each. So these '$100-MILLION DOLLAR

WORKSHOPS' really are worth every penny of the regular price of $3,985.00 each. That's a full $159,400.00 in value for all 40 Workshops. But you can attend as many as you'd like for only your travel expenses (travel, hotel, meals, etc.). That's up to $159,400.00 in real money-making help that you will receive over the next 4 years!

Can't make it to these Workshops? No problem. You can listen in by telephone — or in some cases, log onto the Internet and watch them live. You will be able to participate by phone or on the Internet for some parts of these events. Plus, each wealth-building workshop will be recorded — and you will have exclusive access to each of these private events. This gives you all of the benefits of these valuable life-changing Workshops without leaving the privacy, comfort, and security of your home.

Again, if getting exclusive access to these wealth-building Workshops were all you were receiving over the next 4 years, it would be worth far more than the cost to become a Platinum Member. But wait, the best is still to come...

PLATINUM MEMBER BENEFIT #3:

You will receive the ultimate FREE BONUS GIFT with a real-world value of over $250,000.00!

Section 3 of this book told you all about our Bonus Gift that truly is valued at over a quarter of a million dollars!

Does that _still_ sound hard to believe?

Of course it does! **But if you'll re-read Section 3 of this book, you'll see that this is the gospel truth.** As you'll re-discover, the 300 FREE EBOOK WEB-SITES that will come to you complete with the amazing 'CRM Technology' would easily cost you much more than $250,000.00 if you were to have them built from scratch. But as I proved to you, these really will be given to you absolutely free when you become a Platinum Member of

The experienced mountain climber is not intimidated by a mountain — he is inspired by it. The persistent winner is not discouraged by a problem — he is challenged by it. Mountains are created to be conquered; adversities are designed to be defeated; problems are sent to be solved. It is better to master one mountain than a thousand foothills.

William Arthur Ward

the Direct-Response Network!

These 300 FREE EBOOK WEB-SITES are designed to let up to thousands of other people on the Internet make money for you. They let you cash-in with the most important wealth-making breakthrough the Internet has ever seen! Go back and study this section carefully and you will find yourself shouting, *"Hey, this Free Bonus Gift really is worth over $250,000.00!"* And you'll be right... It really is!

But wait! As great as all this is, there are still 2 more powerful Membership Benefits for you... And each one could be worth a huge fortune to you and your family...

PLATINUM MEMBER BENEFIT #4:

You will receive our highest-level Distributor Position in the Direct-Response Network that is designed to pay you a whopping $2,000.00 cash for every special Membership sale we close for you!

All you do is mail out our magic yellow flyer. That's it! We will take it from there and do our best to close each Membership sale — and rush you a $2,000 Commission check by FedEx. This is our ultimate reward to thank you for becoming a Platinum Member.

All of our other Distributors can only get paid up to $500.00 — but you will be in position to receive up to $2,000.00 cash!

This Member Benefit is based on one important principle:

Those who do more, DESERVE MORE!

Please re-read Section 4 of this book to discover how this works.

Here is a fast summary: When you become a Platinum Member, we will appoint you to the highest Distributor Position in the D.R.N. This puts you in Position to get paid the largest amount of Commission for each Membership we sell to the leads you generate by mailing the magic yellow flyer or letting our experts mail it for you.

Best of all, generating these leads is so simple and easy that a 10 year old child can do it!

How easy? Well, as Section 4 shows you, all you have to do is mail our magic yellow flyer to people who are looking for a way to make huge sums of money. We take it from there and do our best to educate these people on all the ways our various Membership Services can help them make all the money they want and need.

When they join this top-level Membership, we will instantly and send you a Commission check for a whopping $2,000 cash!

But that's only part of the money you can make! You see, we'll also do our best to educate these new Members on all the reasons they should become a Distributor of the D.R.N. And when they do, we will pay you a 100% Matching Bonus check for all the monthly commissions they receive. For example, if we pay them $1,000.00 a month, you get $1,000.00. If we pay them $5,000.00, you get $5,000.00. **This gives you the ultimate way to get up to $2,000.00 cash for each sale we close for you — PLUS receive a huge and growing monthly income that could keep coming to you for many months and perhaps years!**

BUT WAIT: the 5th and final benefit could make you more money than the other 4 benefits combined! *Read on...*

PLATINUM MEMBER BENEFIT #5:

Through our exclusive President's Club, you will become our private Joint Venture Partner — and

have the first chance to cash-in with us whenever we discover something new that we believe has the potential to generate millions of dollars!

This final Platinum Member Benefit is definitely the icing on your get-rich cake!

Remember, we are constantly searching for *'THE NEXT BIG THING'* that could be worth millions of dollars. And when we find it, you'll have the first chance to become our Joint Venture Partner and be in position to cash-in with this new secret. **You will be included with our closest friends who are allowed to come aboard with us and make money with the small and exclusive group of some of the smartest and most talented marketers on the planet!**

How much could you make with this exciting President's Club?

Nobody can say for sure... But there have been times that one of our Joint Venture Partners introduced us to a new opportunity that has ended up being worth millions of dollars to us...

NOW THE SAME THING COULD HAPPEN TO YOU!

As you already know, the world's richest people always include their closest friends whenever they discover a new wealth-making secret or opportunity. This is one of the main reasons why the rich keep getting richer... And now you will have this same powerful wealth making advantage working for you.

So add this up. You'll see. This Platinum Membership really is...

The Ultimate Wealth-Maker!

This Platinum Membership in the D.R.N. gives you the best-of-the-best of the same exact methods, strategies, secrets, close

---

Adversity creates heroes.

Picabo Street

Good timber does not grow with ease; the stronger the wind, the stronger the trees.

J. Willard Marriott

Adversity has the effect of eliciting talents, which, in prosperous circumstances, would have lain dormant.

Horace

personal help, support, and guidance that took us from the small $300.00 ad that launched our company in 1988 — to over $100-Million Dollars in Direct-Response Marketing sales in less than 19 years!

Now these same powerful ingredients that have brought us so many millions of dollars can be the answer to your biggest desires for the wealth that you seek! Please go back through this book to discover more about all the ways these 5 main Platinum Member Benefits can help you make all the money you want, need, and truly deserve. *Then...*

Take Positive Action Today!

Just fill out the Platinum Membership Application Form by going to www.BecomeAPlatinumMember.com — just print out the Application Form — and then return it to us at once. This one small decision could easily turn everything around for you.

An opportunity to get the same tips, tricks, strategies, personal help, support, and continued guidance from a group of dedicated self-made millionaires who have generated tens of millions of dollars from scratch only comes along once in a lifetime, but you have one here... I hope you take it!

ONE FINAL NOTE:

YOUR MULTI-MILLION DOLLAR IDEA IS WAITING!!! Remember the words of Russ von Hoelscher — the man who first made my wife and I millions of dollars — *"All it takes is one idea to make a million dollars!"* It was six months after Russ said these words to us that he did help us turn one simple idea into over one million dollars cash. **Now, we are ready, willing, and able to help you turn one of your ideas (or an idea that we give you!) into well over a million dollars — or more!** It's all right here in the five life-changing Member Benefits you will receive when you become a Platinum Member of our Direct-Response Network. Please hurry — so you can start cashing-in with these 5 main wealth-making benefits!